D1476452

Quashing the Rhetoric of Reform

An Educational Design That Reaches All Children

Eldon Lee
Mary Gale Budzisz

ScarecrowEducation
Lanham, Maryland • Toronto • Oxford
2004

Published in the United States of America
by ScarecrowEducation
An imprint of The Rowman & Littlefield Publishing Group, Inc.
4501 Forbes Boulevard, Suite 200, Lanham, Maryland 20706
www.scaroweducation.com

PO Box 317
Oxford
OX2 9RU, UK

British Library Cataloguing in Publication Information Available

Library of Congress Cataloging-in-Publication Data

Lee, Eldon, 1942–
  Quashing the rhetoric of reform : an educational design that reaches
all children / Eldon Lee, Mary Gale Budzisz.
    p. cm.
  Includes bibliographical references.
  ISBN 1-57886-034-2 (pbk. : alk. paper)
1. School improvement programs—Wisconsin—Milwaukee—Case studies.
2. Charter schools—Wisconsin—Milwaukee—Case studies. 3. Milwaukee
Village School. I. Budzisz, Mary Gale. II. Title.
LB2822.83.W6 L44 2004
371.01'09775'95—dc21   2003013896

∞™ The paper used in this publication meets the minimum requirements of
American National Standard for Information Sciences—Permanence of
Paper for Printed Library Materials, ANSI/NISO Z39.48-1992.
Manufactured in the United States of America.

To the children who taught us the most:
Pat and Mike Budzisz
Victoria Lee, Elizabeth Wright, and Traci Rabindran

To our respective spouses who tolerated
our nonsense and encouraged us to stay
at it when we were headed toward the shredder:
Frank Budzisz
Carita Lee

And, especially, to all the Village students and parents
we had the pleasure of serving

To the memory of David Crouthers

Contents

Foreword

At the Milwaukee Village School (MVS), we were prepared for life and further education. We experienced things that students at a regular middle school would not. My best friend, April Love, and I wanted to choose a different middle school, but our parents insisted that we attend MVS. They felt it was close to home, and we could walk to school. My mom, Faith (Johnson) Bugg volunteered at my school every day. She wanted me close to her to keep me on task. I thank her for that, because her being there has allowed me to be successful now.

While attending MVS we learned so much. We learned not only the academics of a usual middle school, but also we learned what it means to be successful in life through programs such as Best Friends and students fighting Alcohol and Other Drug Abuse (AODA). We traveled to many places volunteering, participating in community experiences, and camping outdoors. In our school, a lot of the kids' only opportunity to see other things, besides their neighborhoods, was through MVS.

We initiated the proficiency checklist and showed the whole Milwaukee, Wisconsin, public school system that it's not only the letter grades that show a person has learned. You have to see that a person has learned the required information. We actually checked off that piece of information learned whenever it was completed. That way you don't get kids sliding through the cracks and failing later in life. You'll know that they really know what they are doing.

MVS has prepared me in many ways. When I left MVS to go to Milwaukee Vincent High School, I was ranked fifth in my class with a 3.8

cumulative grade point average, I was National Honor Society president and elected to the student council, senior board, and Renaissance Honor Roll Club. I also played volleyball, softball, track, and basketball. I was ranked among the top fifty athletes in the state and received various awards such as all-conference, MVP, leading scorer, and scholar athlete. Those are just of few of the many sport awards I received. I completed over three hundred hours of community service in my senior year alone; my previous years in high school would add up to many more. For my numerous hours of community service, I received the United States of America Volunteer Scholarship.

I attend the University of Wisconsin (UW), Green Bay, with an above 3.0 cumulative grade point average. I received fourteen academic scholarships in order to pay for my schooling and also was eligible for many basketball scholarships at various schools. At UW, Green Bay, I am on the Black Student Union, and I am the university reservationist coordinator-supervisor.

Without MVS, my family, friends, and God, I think the foundation would have not been laid to make me a very successful person. April Love and I have turned out to be true products of MVS. I hope you enjoy reading about our experiences.

—Chante Strelke (former MVS student)

Preface

On February 22, 1995, after four hard years of preparation and facing every obstacle imaginable, the Milwaukee Village School (MVS) became a reality. This innovative Milwaukee, Wisconsin, public school was different in every way. It was designed for children, without thought to the wide range of adult influences perpetrated on them in today's educational environment. Buoyed by a supportive superintendent and a small handful of well-wishers, this project took hold in a neighborhood where children were forgotten commodities and adult agendas dominated. This school was designed to educate the whole child.

In this book we, as grassroots people, talk about things we actually did and a few things we wanted to do to change the way we educate children. We include information for educators that can be easily extracted and replicated in their schools. Readers at every level will come away with new, creative ideas that work and will have a renewed sense of how to implement true reform.

This philosophy completely changes the educational design of a middle school to take children "from where they are" toward maximum achievement at their maximum rate, emphasizing their real needs in order to become productive as members of their community and workers on the job in addition to maintaining a household. We encourage our readers to find learning where it is happening, be it in the classroom, in the community, or on the road throughout the country. As we recognized that children learn in different ways and at different rates, it only made sense to respond with a school designed with that in mind.

In our philosophy, we completely change the way we think about providing services to children with special educational needs. When schools are designed for children, they serve all children with a wide variety of needs. In our philosophy, all children enter school simply as children; then, we look at their needs and meet them in a unique, legal way.

As a timely book, this volume can impact such innovations as charter schools, alternative schools, and the new middle and high schools that are currently expanding throughout the country. It will also encourage the implementation of creative ideas in existing schools. Sit back, relax, and take this seven-year journey with us as we build the Milwaukee Village School and Community Center.

This book, written by those in the trenches, documents a complete educational philosophy and the development of a school from beginning to end. The school was designed to respect the intelligence and abilities of all children.

Acknowledgments

A special thanks to those who helped and encouraged us to complete this book: Dr. Ed Pino, Dr. Bob Pavlik, Susan Ohanian, Marie Heiss, David Powell, Jean Heider, Dusty Rose, and the zillions of people who helped the school get off the ground. The dream still lives in this book!

Contact us at Reformers@wholechildreform.com; website www .wholechildreform.com.

All student names are fictitious with the exception of Chante Strelke, April Love, Prince Starnes, Willie Monroe, Ngozie Omegbu, and Wanita Starnes.

CHAPTER 1

Reflections, Comparisons, and Confronting Our Fears

The modern-day system of education was designed in the eighteenth century, when not everyone went to school, and many of those who went didn't complete the minimal education offered. Designed to maintain the status quo, education was seen as unnecessary for those left behind, as they were relegated to the limited work roles of their parents. When he talked about "raking a few geniuses from the rubbish," Thomas Jefferson not only referred to those who were selected to continue their educations, but accurately described the elitist attitudes of that era. Those handpicked students, selected by race and gender, literally learned at the same rate and in the same way in order to fit into the same tiny mold, as dictated by the standards of the time.

Today, according to author John Merrow, we continue "our mad (and doomed) rush to find a single measure of school and student quality," that same tiny mold where only the elite survive (p. 3). Do we truly want a surgeon who is merely adept at a multiple-choice test? Of course not; we want one who can demonstrate the ability to do the job. Then, why do we accept anything less for other skills? How can we truly determine the skills of a student unless we assess in a way that is meaningful, assess in a way that will give significant feedback to teachers, parents, and students and really help the learning process. Clearly, the measure of student quality must be diverse and will increase in range as the child develops interests and seeks out his or her passion in life. With this, the measure of school quality changes dramatically to reflect how it is helping the child progress toward his or her goals, rather than the aforementioned single unit of measurement.

As we abandon the bigotry of the past, recognizing the greater complexity of today's society, it becomes essential for all children to develop a wide range of skills. They must be able to analyze, communicate, and develop thinking skills, leadership skills, and everyday-living skills, all of which are necessary to sustain quality of life and become contributing members of their communities. To ensure that all children reach their maximum potential, educators must recognize differences in learning styles, both in how children learn and how they demonstrate learning. We must recognize, as Dr. Howard Gardner did with his study of multiple intelligences in *Frames of Mind*, that children have different strengths, but more importantly, they have individual interests that we must not continue to restrict with a narrow standard. This narrow standard not only forces children away from their strengths, but also restricts the futures of those who would follow the lead of Albert Einstein, Marion Anderson, Matthew Henson, or Isaac Newton, as these students can no longer reach for their dreams.

How do we accomplish this? How do we break the mold that limits learning and restricts the progress of all children? We start by storming the Bastille of learning, the prison that confines children to the classroom, forced to the drudgery of reading dull textbooks and listening to talking heads. Learning must connect with reality, as community members come into the school and students go out into the community in search of teachable moments. A reality in learning must be developed that allows children to experiment without the fear of failure and to expand their minds to the stars and beyond in search of their passion, their joy of learning. To allow for this, a whole new delivery system for education must be developed.

A significant concern, the differing learning rates of individual children, must also be addressed. Teaching all children from all environments with a whole range of skills does not lend itself to one simple answer. The fact of the matter is, the rigid time frames of the past force failure on children who haven't learned at the same rate, who haven't quite learned, or rather, memorized everything necessary by the day grades are due. Education must be redesigned for children to progress from where they are, taking charge of their educational lives to improve at their own best rates. Simply put, educators can no longer give up on children, as they do today, at the end of every grade period. We must hang on to every child until he or she succeeds, no matter when the child succeeds. The aforementioned tiny mold must be smashed to smithereens. The myth that children must progress and learn in robotic sameness must be dispelled. Education must be for all children.

Everyone is talking about educational reform, but when the words are put into action, the result is a warmed-over version of the same education design that has failed over and over again, rendering these words just more empty rhetoric. This book, however, has no interest in the rhetoric of reform. We speak not from the radio talk show with a political agenda to sell, not from school boards with egos to maintain, not from politicians with their lust for power. We simply speak of the grassroots agenda of children, learned from listening to them and their parents. Instead of issuing edicts from boardrooms or ivory towers as to what should be done, we plan to present what we did. We did it in the community with parents, invested community members, teachers, and children. It wasn't always pretty, but we weren't out simply to patch the crumbling eighteenth-century infrastructure of education. We were out to replace it with a twenty-first-century design that encourages all children to expand their minds to their ultimate capacity. In order to understand our thoughts fully, it is necessary to erase from the mind completely, in the words of veteran seventh-grade teacher James Herndon, "how schools are spozed to be." Imagine schools the way they could be, designed to arm children with the ultimate weapon to enhance their futures, the joy of learning. To accomplish this we must reject those who spew out the rhetoric of reform and embrace those who have the courage to dive headfirst into real reform.

HOW A PRINCIPAL LOSES CONTROL OF HIS SCHOOL AND BRAGS ABOUT IT

Essential to the development of innovative ideas is the ability of teachers to take charge of their educational lives. We must free them from a structure that stifles flexibility and from a wide range of meaningless rules designed to support someone's desire for power and control. We look at some of our experiences to see what we can do to change the way we look at education.

We took away the rules in September 1989 as teacher Mary Gale Budzisz entered my (EL's) alternative school like a Tasmanian devil, initiating creative ideas one after another. The results were phenomenal. She and the students had banned me from a vacant room in the school for over a month, when a young man in a tuxedo came into my office. He bore a slight resemblance to one of my students, but I wasn't sure. He entered and said, "Mr. Lee, I would like to formally invite you to our class play to be held in Room 303."

"Is that you, Marvin?" I asked in bewilderment. Then I collected my wits and formally accepted his invitation. Was this the same Marvin who was continuously in trouble? Continuously acting out? Kinda looked like him. Upon entering the room, I saw a complete set, including a large boat, filling the room. The students had built the whole set and had written, produced, and were about to act in a play that was open to the public by invitation. Students with severe emotional problems, who had made minimal achievements in the past, were learning to write the script, read the script, measure items for the set, do oral presentations, create artistically, coordinate the process, and work as a team to present the play. Marvin was in his tux welcoming all, and the play was set to begin. I knew then that I, as lead administrator, was beginning to lose control of the school! What a wonderful feeling!

With this teacher free to teach, students were allowed to take charge of their educational lives, and they enjoyed it. Now, don't think for a moment this was just playtime or casual learning. These students were expected to learn, and this expectation was reinforced at the beginning and end of every day. When parents wanted to know what their child had learned, Ms. Budzisz was ready to tell them. A strong focus in my (MGB's) class requires student involvement in a daily routine that reminds them, and their teachers, what they are going to learn and what they have learned. The process starts with goal setting every morning. Stating "this is what we are going to do today" really sets the stage for learning. Daily tasks are documented by students in specially designed assignment notebooks that have check-off spaces for student self-evaluation at the end of each day. Together, teacher and students transform a general assignment into a set of workable goals. Learning, by nature, is fun, but it is not play.

High expectations for students continue, every educational minute is accounted for, and assessment is continuous at the classroom level, giving constant feedback to the teacher. The rhetoric of no child left behind becomes reality by letting children learn and teachers teach.

THE PROFESSORS TAUGHT US WELL

The best lessons for educators are taught by students. The best of these teachers are those students who need us the most. Milwaukee's Craig Alternative School served severely emotionally disturbed middle and high school students who had trouble functioning in any other school setting, or any other place in this world for that matter. As a matter of fact, we learned more during this time than during the entire rest of our careers, with the students as our professors. Some more ideas for change.

Tommy and Charles were sent to my (EL's) office again and again for continuous disruption in the classroom. Now, first we must stop and realize that at this alternative school the class size was nine, supervised by two adults, a teacher, and an educational assistant. In order to get sent to the office, a student had to be BAAAAAD! The teacher was trying to get them to read simple words, as they were learning on the preprimer reading level. Tommy and Charles were not happy. "I ain't doin no mother-fucking kindeygarden words," said Tommy. Charles was carrying on a conversation with the teacher out of my hearing range, but I think the word "bitch" came up somewhere, and the teacher was a man. I got the word list from the teacher and escorted the two to my office where they quieted substantially.

I was desperate to find a way to entertain these hooligans until they settled enough to return to class. I turned on my computer to a word processing program.

"Now Tommy, I want you to read the words to Charles okay? Charles, would you type the words on the computer so I can have a permanent record of the list?"

"Okay Mr. Lee, we'll do that for you."

"Help each other if you have any problems," I said. They began working and I left my office for other duties. Actually, I got busy and forgot they were in there. When I returned an hour later, the room was quiet. Remembering that I had left them there, I became concerned that they had roamed and were up to their usual mischief. I asked secretary Diane (Clark) Newton if she had seen them, and she said she hadn't seen or heard them. My concern increased and I rushed into my office only to find Tommy and Charles hard at work, helping each other on the computer.

"We finished the list, Mr. Lee. We put our own words on too," said Tommy.

"And I learned some new words," said Charles proudly.

"You did a wonderful job guys. Thanks," I responded.

Working on the project for over an hour, they had stayed on task, didn't disrupt anyone, read the words without complaint, and wrote the words, and I had the list I wanted for the next time they visited. What a wonderful lesson I had learned; they were the professors, and I was the student. Students were allowed to take charge of their educational lives, doing a task in a different way, working at their own rate and for a specific reason, and they had worked hard to succeed. There were no time lines, no grades, and most importantly, they were not humiliated if they missed a word. They wanted to succeed, they wanted to finish the project, and they taught each other. Now, we, as educators, can take that project and build on it by adding words and increasing their rates, one step at a time, until they reach their goal. Do they really need us to jam education down their throats, using the scare tactics of complete and utter failure if they don't learn? It's time to learn from the professors.

Eighteenth-century education was designed to serve few, while today we must teach all children.

A GLIMMER OF HOPE

Middle school teachers Rose Riege, Monica Moe, and Barbara Kieman, working with Gerard Randle at Milwaukee's Bell Middle School, tried to make a difference. Encouraged by their success, we looked to them for words of wisdom.

Realizing that some urban students had not felt much success in the past, we set about integrating important skills with thematic teaching. Research on best practices indicates that most people need to hear, manipulate, or experience a skill no fewer than seven times before mastering it, so we knew that our students would need the most powerful and natural form of learning: experiential. We set about balancing the curricular content with creative activities that captured the sixth-grader's imagination. "Less is more" became a guiding principle, as the teachers believed the learning emphasis should be on quality rather than quantity, on understanding rather than memorization, and especially on how thinking skills and analytical connections between various specific topics would engage students and motivate them to want to learn more. One example was the Dinosaur Unit. In this unit of study, students taped the hallway with the lengths of various dinosaurs, applying the measurement skills they had learned in mathematics. The teachers incorporated a wide range of reading and writing opportunities, including a creative writing assignment titled "If Dinosaurs Roamed the Earth Today." They read a variety of stories about dinosaurs in reading class to learn the vocabulary of this theme. In science, they classified dinosaurs after studying their habitats, eating habits, and characteristics. Macaulay's *Motel of the Mysteries* captured their imaginations as they became student archaeologists. Field trips to the local community college introduced the students to future employment opportunities in design and welding, as the team of students designed a dinosaur sculpture. With the help of local college students, these youngsters saw their plans and hard work come to fruition as they built a dinosaur sculpture in the courtyard of the school.

They learned welding techniques and the importance of mathematics skills in the outside world. The culmination of the unit included a half-day Dinosaur Dig, where students worked in teams to measure, grid, locate, record, and carefully try to put the bones of a mystery dinosaur together. They became true archaeologists.

Immersing the students in creative, fun, and rewarding experiences allowed them to understand how the materials they were reading and the skills they were learning were authentic and could be used in the outside world. The students began to feel, some for the first time in their lives, a measure of success. Projects and hands-on activities gave a feeling of reality to daily lessons, and quality assessment made the team a good model to follow. Reality struck, however, when we realized many of these students would not graduate. Regardless of how much they had learned, the system was controlled by meaningless standards and time frames conducive to failure. This had to change.

THE HURRIEDER YOU GO, THE BEHINDER YOU GET

As educators serving children in the middle years, we found ourselves quite literally in the middle of a mess. Student failure rates were high, promotion rates were low, and an alarming number of students was dropping out during eighth grade. Not being the type to sit on our hands and watch disaster unfold, we decided to identify obstacles to their success.

Robert has difficulty with math; in fact, he is failing at the end of the first six-week grading period. So, in all our wisdom, what do we do? We go on to the next six-week session and a new group of lessons, completely ignoring the fact that Robert is missing valuable information and skills. This problem continues and gets even worse as he passes the next six-week period with a final grade of D–.

Drastically missing information needed to build skills, Robert falls further and further behind. As a matter of fact, Robert continues to fail throughout the entire year, until he fails the course, which forces him back to the beginning to do it all over again. It's like running a mile race on a quarter-mile track: a runner lags behind after the first lap, fails, and is sent back to the beginning. Now, instead of being a little behind, because the runner has had to repeat the whole lap, he or she is out of contention.

Some schools require passing letter grades for promotion, while others have different standards. Either way, if Robert fails enough subjects or does not attain these standards on schedule, he fails the whole grade and must repeat everything. This cycle goes on until he reaches the age of social promotion. A school in Michigan set this age at fourteen, then encourages failing students to attend an alternative school. Another in Wisconsin made the age fifteen, but either way, once behind, students don't have a chance.

Upon entering high school at the social promotion age of fifteen, Jessica struggles with her ninth-grade textbooks, as she still has extremely poor reading skills. Despite remedial reading classes, or because of them, she cannot make the huge jump necessary to keep pace in most of her classes. At the end of the year, she lacks sufficient credits, making her ineligible for sophomore status. When she returns for her second freshman year at age sixteen, Jessica becomes aware that she is unlikely to graduate before the age of twenty. Even if her grades improve during this year, she is older and hope is dwindling.

One urban high school in Wisconsin was reported to have 550 freshmen students, of which as many as 400 had failed and were attending ninth-grade classes for the second year. At another, 92 percent of those who failed to make sophomore status were African American, comprising 60 percent of the school. The statistics throughout urban systems across this nation indicate nearly half of all students don't graduate. This is the norm for urban schools as they try to meet the needs of today's students in today's world using the educational practices and boundaries of the eighteenth century.

TAKING THE LEAP OF FAITH

"We are still trying to develop both the philosophy as well as a system of education which really does respect the intelligence and abilities of ordinary people." This statement by historian James Anderson underlines the need for massive educational changes and defines the mission for those of us who are unwilling to sit by helplessly. Taking our past experiences, we prepared to move ahead.

Frustration with the current system of education and the damage it does to children was our motivation. The year was 1991 and the seeds of the Milwaukee Village School and Community Center were planted and began to grow. The decision to take on the challenge of school reform is difficult at best. The implementation of the massive changes necessary to reform a school system is a monumental task and will often meet with unbelievable resistance. On a personal level it would take more time and effort than most people want to give. The alternative, however, is to watch children fail, year in and year out, in a system that doesn't seem to give a damn about their success.

Teacher extraordinaire Mary Gale Budzisz agreed to partner with me (EL) on the development of a new middle-high school. We started our campaign by contacting newly appointed Milwaukee Public School (MPS) superintendent Dr. Howard Fuller. In a letter of December 12, 1991, I expressed my desire to change the way we educate children, while Mary Gale, in her own inimitable style, walked right past his executive secretary into the new superintendent's office, sat on his couch, and made herself comfortable. Encouraged by Mary Gale's conversation, Dr. Fuller and I agreed the only way to implement our ideas was to design a new school from the beginning.

We developed a rough draft of our school proposal and sent it to Dr. Fuller for review. Rarely does a superintendent in a large urban school respond to individual thoughts, but we were hoping he would refer it to someone who would. In less than a month, a letter from the superintendent's office appeared in my (EL's) mailbox. Surprised and excited, we read his supportive, yet challenging, response stating, "Your proposal strikes in the right direction generally. You might reexamine it in light of certain elements absolutely critical to an educational plan." In addition, he apologized for taking so long to reply. It was especially significant that he hadn't referred it to anyone else. Thus, the dialogue began. We responded to Dr. Fuller, and he wrote back saying, "You are to be applauded for your obvious concern and commitment to our youth and for the imaginative and creative concepts that you have identified to meet their needs." He then reminded us of the tough road ahead. "Paradigm shifts of this nature are incredibly complex and demand unprecedented levels of energy and commitment by all of us in the educational enterprise." His encouraging comments were a turning point; we knew his support would be strong.

Begin the journey by finding someone of influence. Force yourself on that person, and don't take no for an answer. It's amazing how much they appreciate that, if they are for children.

FORMING COMMUNITIES OF KINDRED MINDS

When the door opens a crack, stick your foot in and never let the door close. Our next goal was to sell our ideas and gather new thoughts in the effort to gain sufficient support to give the proposal credibility. Confronting our fears about the difficulty of the task ahead, we looked to the needs of the children and the support of a broad base of those who were familiar with real reform. Dr. Ed Pino, author and school innovator, clearly shared our views in his book *Remaking Our Schools*:

> We should not organize the curriculum around so many minutes and hours of "sitting time" or around disconnected pieces of content. We should not organize the curriculum around course inputs that are then measured by a "final examination," hence to be quickly forgotten and never revisited for prolonged retention and mastery. We should not organize the curriculum around "grade level hurdles." . . . [T]his idea of student placement has very little to do with how or when students learn. Instead the curriculum should be packaged into many integrated units around broad themes. Students should move along (not [be] promoted) as they master each unit. (p. 134)

Dr. Pino was more than happy to team with us to get the process started. With his support, we actually began to believe we could build a school.

Having no interest in the rhetoric of reform, we proceeded by creating a philosophy, founded on a combination of writings and experiences, and developing it into a proposal. There is minimal precedent for this broad-based systemic change, making evident the necessity to seek the assistance of a whole range of creative minds. Joining Dr. Pino were two former colleagues of mine (EL's) who were well connected in their communities and supportive of grassroots involvement in schools. Our interim board of advisors began with coworkers Bill Brooks and Shirley Harley. A diverse group being essential to the development of a school, we looked to the wisdom of Dr. Nomsa Gwalla-Ogisi, associate professor of special education, University of Wisconsin, Whitewater. Reacting to the Village School proposal, Dr. Gwalla-Ogisi wrote, "Curriculum and program goals are . . . supported by community and school generated realities and would more likely be supported. Partnering with Milwaukee's Bell Middle School, Marquette Electronics Inc. was involved in a wonderful program that brought students into their business as well as employees into the school." Personnel director and coordinator of that project, Guy Hoppe, brought one perspective of business to our board. "What you are proposing is a formula for success, because it empowers teachers and allows addressing needs, school by school."

The CEO of Talisman Press had difficulty getting through high school, but no problem running his company. Bob Ryan's vision for the school was told through a story about a young man who visited his shop regularly:

> This child has gotten virtually nothing out of his schooling. . . . A school such as the one in this proposal would embrace a child like that, find his strengths and build on them as he wins daily, instead of losing. His self-esteem would grow as he accomplishes things he wasn't sure he could do. His confidence would spill over into everything he does.

This is the beginning of the broad-based support system necessary to share ideas, as well as to network the community for systemic change.

As we spent many hours consulting with students and parents alike, we developed a grassroots perspective and an honest-eye view of what was happening. To build a strong base, we sought a wide and diverse range of partners within the community we were about to enter. Included were former principals and teachers, YMCA personnel, local support agencies, judges, lawyers, ministers, block clubs, local politicians, and anyone else who would support the program by becoming actively involved. We were amazed at how many came on board. No one ever said no.

The steam engine was going full throttle in an effort to get the support of the whole village. Vaughn Beals, former CEO and part owner of the Milwaukee-based Harley-Davidson Company, summed it up quite well when he reminded us that everyone truly wanted the same thing for children and, if we focused on that, we would do well. Harley-Davidson was well known for its teamwork with labor.

Following his advice, our next step was to approach the teachers' union, the Milwaukee Teachers' Education Association (MTEA), to solicit their support. Historically, this organization had not been particularly friendly to dramatic change. They did, however, go hand in hand in support of innovative ideas presented for Hi Mount School. Principal Spence Korte developed an innovative program that gave more autonomy to individual schools in a large urban system, and the union had stood beside Dr. Korte when the proposal was presented to the board. This was an encouraging first step, but would they be as receptive to our massive reform as they were to Dr. Korte's program?

Proposal in hand, we marched on April 26, 1994, into the Milwaukee teachers' union office for our first meeting. The proposal represented over two long years of preparation and breaking down barriers, yet we had a long way to go. As a teachers' union member, Mary Gale took the lead. Almost too quickly, their representative agreed to move our proposal forward through their process. A union representative presented the proposal to the teachers' union executive board and at their teachers' assembly. It was then faxed to the Wisconsin state union headquarters, and copies were distributed to teachers' union members, many of whom were quite enthusiastic about it. Surprised and even stunned at the response of the union, we wondered, Why the big change? Certainly credit was due for their support, but we understood politics more than most people thought. If the truth be known, in past years, the union would not have supported ours or any other proposal. Confirming this, a union representative indicated that when the private firm the Edison Project threatened to gain access and bring private education into the system, the political climate changed rapidly. Edison was a private for-profit company going nationwide, promising a better education for children if Edison could administer a school. The union, of course, would not be involved in the process. Many saw privatization as a way to get rid of costly union contracts. As Edison presented its case, union officials got nervous; thus, internal reform gained in popularity at an alarming rate. Movement toward real reform had required a severe jolt to the system, and the Edison Project had provided it.

Riding the new wave of reform, support began to pour in from every direction. Politicians, university personnel, and union leaders were among those who were now clamoring to get on board. Remember, we weren't just planning an isolated school; we were planning a complete program designed to educate and support children and the community, and we needed the support of the whole village. We adapted an African proverb to read "it takes a whole village to educate a child" and used it as our slogan.

While promoting your ideas, seek out those who will challenge your thinking and provide a service to your children once your ideas are implemented; then, shake up the system.

THE POLITICS OF THE MALL

Draft proposal in hand, we encountered a bureaucratic nightmare when we discovered there was no process within the school system to get it heard by the Milwaukee Board of School Directors. That school board operates independently of the superintendent, and its members must approve projects of this size before they can proceed any further. It's hard to imagine a large urban school system with many bright and creative employees and no way for their voices to penetrate the fortress-like walls of central administration, even with the support of the superintendent. Drastic measures were needed. We followed the advice of folk musician Dave Guard, given when fellow musician Brownie MacIntosh asked him how to help promote his latest CD: "Drop 'em from airplanes Cap'n, drop 'em from airplanes." So we dropped our proposal from airplanes and took it everywhere.

We knocked on the doors of board members like Dave DeBruin to discuss the Village School proposal. We were having second thoughts, but Dave's encouragement helped us to stay the course. By networking with as many individual board members as possible, one can get a feel for the mood of the whole board and its willingness to consider changes. In the midst of all this, I (EL) had an opportunity to attend a second interview for the position of principal of Juneau High School in Milwaukee. Sharing this with Dave, I confided I wasn't sure I even wanted to go, but he reminded me that this interview would be a remarkable opportunity to talk about the Village School proposal. During the interview, questions were asked about the high school, but my answers were about the Village philosophy. I'm sure the hiring committee was confused, but at the end of the interview, I pulled out the Village School proposal and said, "This is what I want to do." I excused myself and went back to work on the proposal.

Use every opportunity to promote your proposal. Knock on every door.

Time flew by and, with desperation, we knocked on doors and networked, intending either to get our point across or make people sick of seeing us. We were not sure which prevailed, but finally our proposal was sent to the school board committee for review. After long discussion and intense scrutiny, that committee confirmed that "there was no official process to recognize the proposal." Aaaaargh!

Exasperated, we referred the proposal to Superintendent Fuller as a "school board–initiated charter school." Charter schools, however, were not legal at that time in Wisconsin, so the proposal had to go back through the school board, following the original process. Reaching yet another dead-end, we wondered why we didn't give up. Enough was enough; we were going around in circles.

A chance encounter with school board president Mary Bills in Milwaukee's Grand Avenue Mall provided an unexpected opportunity for me (EL) to vent my frustration. She could see the desperation in my eyes, a crazed school administrator ready to kidnap the board president and hold her for ransom to get his proposal heard. She thought for a minute. "What if we had an innovative schools process designed to hear proposals such as yours? Maybe an innovative schools committee could be formed to encourage more creative ideas." I calmly responded, "Great idea, Mary," and quietly walked away. Isn't it amazing how much can be accomplished away from offices in the middle of a mall?

Action was quick as the board approved an Innovative Schools Committee, as well as a procedure to encourage the future implementation of new ideas throughout the system. This major step forward was followed by policies, procedures, and even money for the development of the proposal. That's not all. Upon approval there was money for implementation of the proposal and money for supplies and materials. We moved rapidly, entering our proposal into the process on August 9, 1994. Now let's get out our calculators. Remember, it was December 12, 1991, when we first talked to Dr. Fuller about the project. It was now August 9, 1994. During that time, every day had been utilized talking, planning, and networking our ideas. Yes, we were determined that the proposal would succeed. There was no turning back now.

Network, network, network! Take your proposals and drop 'em from airplanes, Cap'n. Just when you think all is lost, someone who believes in children will come through.

Working on the fast track, it was not long before we were addressing the twenty-five or so professionals, parents, and community members forming the Innovative Schools Committee brought together to review proposals. The concept of school innovation was beginning to catch on, and we found ourselves in the good company of fellow presenters like Sallie Brown and her innovative program, the Wisconsin Conservatory of Life-Long Learning, Tom McGinnity and his Plymouth Institute/High Wind Learning Center, and John Polczynski and his Milwaukee School of Entrepreneurship.

Our presentation, brief and to the point, left us with a good feeling, which was substantiated within a week when we received notice that the committee "unanimously recommended support of the further development of the proposal."

With a small budget, a borrowed office, and several weeks to prepare, we frantically proceeded toward our next step: the final completed proposal. Freed from our daily duties, our full focus was on the project. We wrote and rewrote and rewrote again, sharing ideas with all we met. Again, we spent hours and hours talking to others with varying ideas. A daily update was sent to all interim board members, and information was coming in from everywhere. With the proposal completed, we eagerly awaited the next Innovative Schools Committee meeting for final approval of our program.

Time went by, and either we weren't notified or we just plain missed that all-important meeting; it was held without us. Arlene Sershon, the staff member in charge of the committee, called and asked, "Why weren't you there to present?" After a brief explanation and an offer to come right over, she stepped away from the phone for a minute and replied, "Never mind, I'll let you know." With time getting short and three years of hard work at stake, our frustration mounted. The thought of the proposal being put off for another year was devastating.

Daily routine had taken over, and I (EL) was busy with the mundane problems of the moment when our school secretary interrupted and handed me a pink slip. "Here's a message from Arlene Sershon," she said soberly. My heart in my throat, I slowly peeked at the note and read one word at a time. "Your proposal was . . ." I stopped there for a moment. Would it say rejected? Would it say put off until next year? "Your proposal was approved unanimously by the Committee." I jumped up and down in my mind. My body, however, was slumped in a chair with a big smile on my face. I pulled up some energy and ran, not walked, over to Mary Gale's classroom to let her know the good news. "We did it. We're on the way." We had one more obstacle to overcome, and MVS would be a reality. The full monthly school board meeting was to be held February 22, 1995.

Developing a proposal for a new school takes hours and hours of knocking on doors and brainstorming ideas with those whose focus is on children. This takes an enormous amount of energy.

CHAPTER 2

Headline: "Ant Moves Rubber Tree Plant"

DIVING HEADFIRST THROUGH THE WINDOW OF OPPORTUNITY

Since it took two hundred years of hard work to develop an elitist school system, it is clear that an enormous amount of time and energy will be necessary to change it. Whether starting a new school or changing an existing one, those who challenge the status quo find an obscene number of obstacles in their path. Look at the enormous amounts of reform rhetoric spewed out over the past twenty years; all that has been accomplished is the equivalent of reshuffling the deck chairs on the Titanic. As a matter of fact, making sporadic changes to an existing school is of little or no value. A statement made by Joe Garba, recently retired dean of education at Hamlin University in Minnesota, reinforces this view:

> I often think that while almost everyone in this country wants our schools to be better, almost nobody wants them to be different. But I really don't believe we can have the kind of schools we need in the 21st century if we aren't willing to make them significantly different from the schools that we had in the 20th century. And I don't believe we can get the kind of schools we need by changing the ones we've got.

This is a call for us to refocus our priorities. We must start over by asking the fundamental questions, Who matters? Whom are we developing schools for? With these questions, we roll up our sleeves and shout to the educational world, "Give us your best shot, 'cause here we come! We are here to develop a school for children."

Making the needed dramatic change not only requires a new approach inside the building, but a whole new philosophy regarding the involvement of the surrounding community. Essential to a successful school philosophy is developing a concept where students can explore the school neighborhood and their home neighborhood simultaneously, where those parents coming in and out of the school are also neighbors. The new concept embraces a kind of learning not perpetuated by expensive gimmicks in the classroom, but supported by the quality, reality, and easy access of the community. The journey to this community and true educational reform takes a rough road fraught with obstacles that could not have been imagined by those who truly believe in children.

We began our search for a location to start the new MVS. A study of the demographics led us to an area heavily populated by youth in the desired age range. We hopped into the car and drove through back alleys to locate vacant buildings. At an abandoned church connected to a building formerly housing a private school, we met some fascinating people, including a dedicated woman running a clothing exchange. What a great collaboration this would make: parents and neighbors coming into the exchange, making the building the hub of the community, while students helped in the exchange to improve their math and business skills. The Lisbon Avenue Neighborhood Development Association (LAND), located in the building, reached out to us immediately in an effort to team in the best interest of children. This building was located in an urban neighborhood with a large number of middle school–aged children. We were excited about that location and were ready to open our school wherever we could serve children. We met with the director of LAND and were invited to present our plan to a local community steering committee.

Committee members attending included John, who worked at the local junior college, and Victor and Martha, who lived in the building we wished to inhabit; the committee was chaired by the director, Ms. Twomey. As we approached the meeting, we wondered what questions awaited us. We were anxious to hear what educational concerns they had. We presented our program to the committee, expressing clearly our interest in the well-being of children. We were surprised by the directness and tone of their questions, as the once friendly atmosphere turned negative.

"Why are you here?" asked Victor abruptly.

"Why do you want to come from the suburbs to work with our children?" asked John.

We answered, but the tone and demeanor remained negative and the racial references clear. Having worked in urban areas most of our lives, this was something we weren't used to. The subject of children didn't seem to enter their conversation, so we prepared to abandon this effort. To this day, their attitude still remains a mystery, but we were clearly aware of sabotage efforts among those who claimed dictatorship of a community.

Our welcome to the world of innovative education continued. Our main objective was to give public school parents a choice, a different way to educate their children. With this in mind, we expected a groundswell of support from those who advocated the "school choice" program. After all, didn't we want the same thing: a choice for parents and children?

Well, this was where the rhetoric came out into the open. Without ever talking to us, a local "choice" advocate made it clear we were not welcome in her neighborhood. She sent a note intended for the governor, stating that we were a bunch of white people coming to their neighborhood to tell black people what to do. We doubted that this message was from parents of potential students in the area, nor did we believe it was based on a survey of neighborhood residents. Was it the solo voice of a politician speaking her rhetoric, regardless of her constituents? Too many politicians lack faith in and respect for those neighborhood parents who might want to make their own decisions. Regardless of the reason, she went to great lengths to oppose us. This racial smokescreen falls far from the truth that the real agenda was based on issues of power, ego, and control.

To defuse all adult agendas, we put our fate in the hands of superintendent Dr. Howard Fuller and were willing to go wherever he placed us to serve children. With the new school year almost upon us, he made the decision to place us in his old alma mater, North Division High School.

The question always becomes, Who matters? Who are we building schools for? Who really forms the welcoming committee for a new school and new ideas?

Beware of self-appointed community leaders and politicians who act independently of their constituents. Their agenda may be based on issues of power, ego, and control, rather than the best interest of children.

Having been rejected by self-appointed community leaders and self-serving politicians, we wondered about the attitude of the parents of students the school would serve. Would they reject or welcome our new school and us? We decided it was important to find out.

In the name of fairness, we took to the streets in our newly acquired neighborhood to meet parents and enroll children. These parents, so often ignored by self-appointed community leaders, would decide if they wanted to send their children to our school. They would make the decision whether our school would exist. We got a list of all addresses, sent out flyers, and started knocking on doors. Soon we discovered there weren't many doors to knock on; some houses just weren't there anymore in this transient urban neighborhood. When we did find a house, quite often the original occupants had moved. After riding in circles, community aide Shirley Harley said, "To hell with the addresses" and pointed out a group of children playing in one of the yards. As they appeared to be of middle school age, we approached them and asked if we could talk to their parents. Welcomed at every stop, we soon discovered that most of these children were not yet enrolled in school. Our first two stops had us enrolling two children, and we were on our way. Riding around some more, we noticed several children standing near a house. We knocked on the door and were welcomed in by Ms. Starnes.

"Boy am I glad to see you," she said. "I wanted a school where my son, Prince, could walk to so I can keep track of him, and your school is only four blocks away."

She went to the hall to call upstairs. Her mother lived upstairs, and two more middle school–aged children were enrolled in the living room of that one house. Upon leaving, we were directed down the street to the house of their cousin, who also didn't have a school. His mother welcomed us with open arms.

The next day in the neighborhood, children came up to us asking, "Are you the ones starting the new school?"

"Yes," we said.

"I want to come. Can I come to your school?" they asked. Upon receiving our flyer, parent Faith (Johnson) Bugg came running over to enroll her daughter Chante and Chante's friend April. They had just been assigned to a magnate school, but really wanted to go to school in the neighborhood. Ms. Bugg was in our school daily, supporting her child, who, seven years later, graduated with honors from a public high school, as did April.

Although we didn't get the 120 students we wanted, we were satisfied with the 88 we did get. It was a good number to start with, and from that year forward, we packed the house. This was a most fascinating summer; our original staff members—social worker Bill Brooks, community aide Shirley Harley, Oxford graduate student Trina Williams, Mary Gale, and I (EL)—were welcomed into homes wherever we went. We developed a wonderful attachment to the newfound parents and brought on board more invested community members. There was no doubt that the real community was receptive. This real community, whose members' voices are too often silenced, now had a booming voice.

Who matters? The children and parents matter the most, and it's time they had their say. How could anyone argue against the school these neighborhood parents chose for their children?

For support, go to the neighborhood, knock on doors, and talk to the invested community members, the parents whose children will attend your school.

COEXISTING: A TWENTY-FIRST CENTURY SCHOOL IN AN EIGHTEENTH-CENTURY WORLD

In this day of increasing needs and diminishing money, it becomes necessary to be creative in every way. Urban areas are riddled with half-empty high school buildings, wasting not only square footage, but also wonderful learning opportunities. Imagine for a moment several small high schools operating independently with their students teaming with middle school students to teach and learn higher-level skills. Imagine middle school students entering a high school that has become completely familiar, providing the comfort level that leads to success. Acting together as a cooperative team, these schools would operate separately, but also team together for the best interests of all.

How do we accomplish this feat? How do we get two schools to operate within one building? Again, every obstacle will be thrown into the path of those who stand for the agenda of children. Guy Hoppe of Marquette Electronics, an original board member, wrote a letter warning us about coexisting in one building: "Don't try this in an existing school building, because I believe you would set up a competitive situation which would not be desirable." How could we make it desirable? We had no other choice; we had to make it work. We took Guy Hoppe's supportive words to heart as we prepared to meet with resistance from more adult agendas, those whose focus was on the needs of the adults, rather than those of the children.

The thought of sharing a building with a traditional high school was not ideal, but we had a home and were ready to move forward. When asked, "Why are you here?" we simply responded, "Dr. Fuller sent us." A school board meeting was held to finalize this placement and I (EL) was there to answer questions. An official from North Division High school was there also. We were told everything was in place; all agreements were set and we had a facility. Or did we? When a board member asked if there was room for MVS at North Division High School, the high school official went up to the microphone and said, "No." Deputy Superintendent Bob Jasna's mouth dropped. There was silence.

Was there no room at the inn for neighborhood children? We had no knowledge of the space situation in the high school, nor had we chosen that location. School board members, however, indicated that the school was highly underutilized and that there was plenty of room. The school board approved our program, but the specifics of our facility were yet to be negotiated with defiant high school authorities.

When the window of opportunity opens a crack, dive in; there's no time to wait for perfection. Get started any way you can, and then pull the pieces together.

Settling into our new home, we knew we had our work cut out for us. As we set up our office on the second floor, we immediately understood why we were placed in the high school. Our first couple of days had us asking, "Where are the kids?" The place was unbelievably empty, as evidenced by a later report by the North Central Regional Evaluation Lab (NCREL), a service of the United States Department of Education:

> Walking into North Division High School on Milwaukee's near north side as the morning bell rings, one's footsteps conspicuously echo in the cavernous hallways. Bracing for the steady drone of student voices, one hears only the occasional voice of the doorway proctor speaking into the hand radio she uses to communicate through seeming miles of hallway coursing through the school.

A decade prior to this, the high school was featured on a nationally televised news report emphasizing the school's poor attendance rate. Not much had changed. Can you imagine only a few children, relatively, being actually served on a multimillion-dollar budget?

> *To allow this financial rape of the taxpayer is inconceivable but not unusual in urban school systems.*

BLENDING IN (YOUR BLENDER OR MINE?)

Reformers find obstacles emerging seemingly out of nowhere, thrown in their path by those who seek to maintain the status quo. Power, ego, and control are the orders of the day, as every effort is made to protect turf and to destroy any chance of change. Immediately recognizing the accuracy of Guy Hoppe's statement, we requested a neutral building manager to oversee utilization of the high school facilities. Our request was denied. We were experiencing the beginning of even more obstacles designed to cling to the failed past.

The struggle for space within the building was long and difficult. Our quest for a physical education facility was met with strong opposition. High school officials stated that they were in charge of the building and that there was no room for our children to do physical education. Those officials indicated our children must use a facility outside the building and suggested the YMCA, which was five blocks away, or the Lutheran church across the street. According to North Division's records, most high school classes were filled with children, but that was the case only on paper. Reality told a different story. A large field house had plenty of room, as did the Olympic-size pool showing nary a ripple in the water as we walked by. One day, I (EL) counted seven students total in the field house. This was not unusual.

After months of trying to build a mutually supportive atmosphere, I was angered at the thought of children being denied access to this wonderful, empty facility. It was time to put my foot down and request the support of central administrative specialists. In a letter to Superintendent Fuller, I wrote:

> I believe their [North Division High School's] efforts are self-serving, unprofessional and destructive to children. It is not conscionable to continue the development of MVS at this time, under these conditions. MVS will not allow our children to be used as pawns in adult power games. We are putting the program on hold until we hear from you.

An immediate response had administrative specialists Therese Campos and Willie Jude acting as referees in the effort to procure at least minimum physical education facilities within the building. Their support garnered us a dirty, dingy utility gym in the basement as a start, but at least it was in the building.

> *All school leaders housed in one building must operate on an equal basis and must work as a team to avoid a hostile environment. Putting an independent building manager in charge of a facility and its day-to-day usage is the first step in developing a workable school within a school.*

As we took the daily walk with our students to the basement gym, we passed the virtually empty field house in the middle of this wonderful facility. The students responded.

"Why can't we use their gym?" asked Aleeyah. "There's no one in there."

"And their pool is empty too," said David. This daily trip to "the back of the bus" inspired us to double our effort to finagle our way upstairs into that field house whenever possible. We initially believed that once we had gotten our feet in the door, the rest would follow. This, however, was not as easy as it sounded; the struggle seemed to go on and on. Allocated minimal space, the next obstacle was access to keys. Where were the keys?

I became the Key Man, running around to unlock rooms with my semimaster, another duty in an already full day. Again, the NCREL report: "North Division officials indicate access to keys is not a condition of the (MVS) occupancy." Keys, easily accessible to retired staff people, were not made available, as the high school maintained its tight control, disregarding the superintendent's wishes. Although each teacher had a key to his or her room, access to keys for other rooms in the area, such as student lavatories, utility rooms, teachers' lavatories, our lunch area, and storage rooms, was limited by the high school. Again, creativity took over, and we got help in strange places. Mary Perry, a recently retired teacher, ran the Modeling Club after school, but more importantly, also had the keys needed to access every room in the area. She was wonderful. But the crap kept coming.

Day after day, high school PA announcements interrupted lessons, blaring information not necessary to our school into all rooms.

"Those interested in going out for the volleyball team will meet in the field house immediately after school," blared the announcements from a speaker by the classroom door.

"Aw shut up," said John.

"They don't even let us in their field house," lamented Julia.

"They don't even want us here," said Mary sadly. A request to have the PA disconnected in our rooms went nowhere; we were told that nothing could be done about it and that we would have to live with it "until we moved out." This called for more creativity. One day I overheard a school engineer talking about how he had cut off his speakers. "The constant interruptions were so irritating I had to cut them off," he said. Sympathetic to us, he loaned us the key needed to access speakers in all of our rooms. The school social worker, Bill Brooks, and I grabbed some wire clippers, and the offending racket was history. Never again did the high school announcements bother us.

How did we overcome obstacles like this? How did we establish ourselves as a school in the building? One step at a time, that's how. Slowly but surely, we made progress with those high school educators who truly cared about children. Initial support was in the form of two retired high school teachers, Mary Perry and Sarah Grant, who welcomed our students to the high school Modeling Club and African Dance Club, respectively. Courageous high school staff members like guidance counselors Terry Trimberger and Marguerite McGill openly supported MVS students, as did social worker Valencia Westmoreland, who was allowed by North Division authorities to sit on our Village Counsel, but only if it was during her lunch hour. The high school librarian, Diane Smith, welcomed our students and our library moms, while a high school Spanish teacher, Kay Bailey, brought her students to our classrooms to teach our children some Spanish. Anna Grosgalvis was also helpful with computer technology. Slowly, we won over the true educators.

> *In a hostile environment gain the confidence of a small number of educators who are supportive. Build on that base. Sometimes, longevity is the key. You win over some, and you simply outlast the others.*

Once in the door, inch by inch, we proceeded to make a home for our students. Starting with a ragtag setup of partitions and shared rooms, we progressed to form our own identity, two years later, by constructing a facility designed for children rather than adults, making students the center of the focus. Over objections from the high school, then superintendent Bob Jasna approved a plan to construct a school within the high school to our specifications. We were fully involved in the planning of this construction, without interference from the high school. Designed to meet the needs of the students and to support innovative ideas, this bold step brought out even more obstacles lurking in the shadows. The plan was to build our new facility on the second floor, replacing the relatively empty high school social studies department. We were excited about the location as it put us near two supportive teachers, Ms. Smith, the high school librarian, and Ms. Grosgalvis, the high school computer specialist. Our threat to enter the sacred halls of the social studies department, however, had teachers in that department up in arms; they were not amused. As a matter of fact, teachers from that department refused to speak to us and wore yellow ribbons for the entire year, mourning the loss of their space.

Several schools within one building is becoming a necessity. No longer can school districts afford to have half-empty buildings while the need for more smaller schools rises. While we need to respect the teachers' desire to be comfortable in their assigned rooms, the building still belongs to the taxpayers, and the primary tenants are the children.

BUILDING OUR HOME

Students, as the most significant tenants of the school building, must drive its usage. How do we create a building for children? How do we make a structure that is friendly to the students and serves their needs? With our full involvement in its design and implementation, that's how. The building-within-a-building design had rooms in close proximity to one another, making it easier for two class teams to work together. These rooms, along with the high school library and our school office, surrounded what used to be an open area used primarily by social studies teachers and the occasional student. This open area became known as the "Village Square," a place for students, parents, and community members to gather for activities. Alive with children throughout the day, this area was available for a variety of activities.

Surrounding the area on the inside of the Square were small rooms designed for no more than twelve to fifteen students. Each team had access to at least one of these rooms for small-group activities. An integral part of the Square was the nurse's area. Our nurse was a mentor, teacher, and leader, and her accessibility to students was essential. One half of the utility room, which had been designed for the utmost efficiency, was set up as a lab area. The other half was equipped with stoves, microwaves, and dishwashers to help teach cooking-related skills built into the integrated curriculum. Certainly not least, our Parent Room served as a workroom used by parents, the parent liaison, and business partners. For six months office staff and teachers worked out of boxes and around the ongoing construction, but it was worth it.

Have no doubt that every inch was well utilized by children, parents, educators, and community members. The school was alive with children and people serving the needs of children.

GET OUT THE TIN CUP

The next major challenge before us was the acquisition of sufficient funding to do all the projects we had planned. While seeking sufficient funding to run a school, we gave strong consideration to begging for money on a street corner, clearly the easiest alternative. The cost of educating children had grown to an all-time high. Politicians were squeezing the dollar tighter. They clearly did not fully recognize the educational needs of children; nor did they realize that these children, as future tax-paying citizens, were a solid financial investment in the future of this country's economy. So we got out our tin cup and headed to the street corner, knowing we were going to need all the help we could get. Grant money, as an answer, often leads to disappointment, as school officials quickly realize that all schools are going for the same pot of money. Thriving on cutthroat politics, education systems offer a special challenge for schools to get on the "most-favored" list of their local, state, or federal grant committees in order to develop their ideas sufficiently.

Attempting to procure a small family/community partnership grant, we sent one of our parents, Melissa Johnson, community representative Theresa Coleman, and psychologist Tim Fosshage to attend a workshop on family-community-school partnership sponsored by the State Division of Public Instruction. As a direct result of that conference, we were chosen as recipients of a $500 seed grant to develop a full community proposal. The money, as in many urban systems, was routed through the local central administration, which, in this case and after all our hard work, arbitrarily decided to use it elsewhere. A small, centralized committee attempted to thwart the efforts of parents and community members alike. Monies distributed in the best interest of the district overshadowed local efforts, clearly trying to sabotage the concept of parent and community involvement. However, we were not to be denied. I (MGB) went into the central office kicking and screaming and came back with our $500. I didn't care if it was ten cents, I was going to get our grant. Lacking most-favored status, networking and continuous grant writing were essential for the financial stability of the school. How did we get past this obstacle and get noticed and accepted in the dog-eat-dog world of procuring funds?

First, we didn't take no for an answer, and then we looked to the children for support.

When we set out to develop a proposal for a much larger service-learning grant offered by the state, we fully involved students in every aspect. This was their grant, and ownership was a major part of our philosophy. Leading the way, Prince and Wanita worked tirelessly to come up with ideas to serve their community, while incorporating all aspects of learning into the activities. Clearly, they got help from adults, but the students led the way. First, they requested student representatives from every class. These representatives sat around an executive board table and brainstormed about the subject, service learning. They talked about the best ways to help their neighbors. When the subject of planting gardens or flowers in the neighborhood came up, all agreed it was a good idea. However, none of the participants had ever planted anything before. It was about time they learned. Small groups gathered, bringing together their ideas, and the result was the writing of a grant proposal with two main objectives: learning how to plant a garden and flowers and actually going out and doing it. The grant proposal was completed and edited by teachers and sent to the state. All students' expectations were exceeded when they received the good news that the concept of their "garden grant" had been accepted. Their excitement carried them to the next stage. A meeting scheduled for all grant recipients across the state had students Andre and Prince nervously preparing their presentation. They were the representatives of MVS. Surrounded by a sea of suits, ties, and titles, they waited for their turn to present their project. Andre seemed a little nervous, but Prince was cool as a cucumber waiting for his turn to go on stage. When their names were called, they walked right up to the microphone as if they owned it. Eleven years old and in charge of the world, they were at their best. It brought tears to my (MGB's) eyes, and they were so proud.

> Look to children as leaders. Put them in the forefront of fund-raising efforts. Have students develop ownership by being fully involved in every aspect of these processes. Have them design and write the grant proposals based on their needs, of course with the support and assistance of educators. Who can tell the story of their needs better than they? When all is done, be sure they are fully prepared, and have them do the presenting.

THE DESPERATE SEARCH FOR TEACHERS OF KINDRED MINDS

Crucial to the development of a school is a team of educators working together to create lessons away from the textbook. Finding the kind of teacher it takes to build this team is much more difficult than it seems in a large urban system. Bright-eyed student teachers anxious to change the world slowly develop into clones of their cooperating teacher after time spent in a textbook-oriented environment. Crushed by a wave of bubble-sheet mania and the memory of their own school years, they are quickly transformed into lemmings jumping into the sea of educational rhetoric. Unable to tread water, many follow its flow, taking the easiest course—textbooks and preprinted curriculums. This makes their journey just a little easier, but less meaningful for students. Supported by mentors who themselves have risen to their positions by seniority rather than vision, their creativity is slowly and methodically siphoned away.

Amazingly, some do slip out of the mold and immediately embark on the rocky road to reform. In these teachers of kindred minds is a true connection to children, along with the creativity to look past antiquated curricular design and find ways to connect learning to their students. These teachers see a walk in the park as an opportunity for a teachable moment, rather than a time to vegetate. They see a stream as a lesson in mathematics, determining the distance across without getting their feet wet. They follow the creatures in the grass or compare vegetation under different conditions and see a lesson in biology, as they connect these experiences to a lesson before they set foot outside the classroom.

Are these teachers born to teach? Are they raised to it as children? Can this way of teaching be taught at all? Is it in all of us, waiting to come out? No one is sure, but essential to reform is turning these visionaries loose on the educational world to see what they can do. There are many teachers, however, who don't understand the true needs of their students. So many balk at reform and are stuck in the never-ending cycle of the status quo. How do we crack the brick wall of entrenchment? One way is by forming communities of kindred minds, bringing them together in one school, and seeing what happens.

Essential to the development of a school is hiring teachers who believe in a creative philosophy.

This sounds absurd to most businesspeople. The hiring process in many large urban systems has central office administrators sitting at their desks deciding in which school newly hired teachers are to be placed. School principals, waiting to see who shows up on their doorstep, have no input, unless of course they have most-favored status. The transfer process between schools in a large system can be even worse. Totally ignoring the necessity of a team atmosphere, administration-union contracts often allow teachers to transfer into a school based on teacher request and seniority. How do we get around this obstacle in a large urban system? How do we get the appropriate teachers?

Every effort should be made to connect the right group of educators to the children they serve. To accomplish this, hiring rules that hinder such access must be examined. It is surprising how many rules aren't rules at all, once one breaks through the line of rhetoric protecting them. In Milwaukee, we followed the lead of then principal Dr. Spence Korte. Hi Mount Elementary School, Milwaukee Public Schools, started the flow of reform by developing a memorandum of understanding (MOU) agreement between the MTEA and school administrators, which allowed them to hire teachers by interview and to receive transfer teachers without regard to seniority. In addition, the MOU allowed for either the teacher or the school principal to initiate a request for transfer from the school if either believed his or her views were inconsistent with the philosophy of the program. This was wonderful, especially with a developing school, and we adopted it also. It was important that we kept teachers who understood and supported the unique philosophy of the school. The winds of change, although not yet a gale, were increasing. Once one school acquired this ability, how could others be refused?

While walking through the halls of the high school, I (EL) overheard a teacher say that North Division High School had an agreement that eliminated limits on the number of African American teachers assigned to the school. A Milwaukee federal court desegregation order allowed a maximum of 23 percent and a minimum of 17 percent of any school staff to be minority. As our school was in a predominantly black neighborhood and we were a neighborhood school, we knew we were going to have a black student population near 100 percent. It only made sense that we had a large populace of the best black teachers available. I immediately contacted the union and the appropriate central administration personnel, and we shortly gained the support of yet another contractual agreement. We were able to procure 70 percent black teachers, as well as 70 percent black support staff, and we maintained that ratio, a valuable asset to the students and the community, throughout our tenure.

System hiring practices must be checked to ensure the acquisition of the best teachers. Especially in the beginning years, the ability to remove those who are not supportive is essential.

Special agreements like the MOUs are helpful, but obstacles remain that affect hiring unless the new rules apply to all schools. Individual agreements serve a purpose as they blaze the trail for much-needed future possibilities; however, they cannot stand alone for long. The third year at MVS found us with several staff openings, plus the addition of five new classes. We interviewed and provided a two-week workshop for a group of interested teachers, but had no assurance they would be able to transfer successfully to our school. Four did transfer successfully, but many did not, due to a variety of rules and games. As an example of the hiring games, a music teacher who had moved her instruments in and attended our two-week summer workshop was denied transfer to MVS. It was alleged that she had not made proper application to the central office. "Excessed" from her current school, meaning she now had no school assignment, she still wasn't allowed to come over and was eventually placed in a high school teaching social studies and music. Another game affected Kathy Jones-Rosa, a certified exceptional education teacher who desperately wanted to join our staff. After a long wait we were told that contractual rules requiring a mandated stay at her current school made her ineligible to transfer. Mark Jabir, whom we originally hired as an educational assistant, was also, at that time, an education student at Marquette University. When it came time for him to student teach, he chose MVS as his assignment. After he fulfilled that assignment, we were interested in hiring him for a special education position. Although he was not certified in special education, he interviewed with us, accepted a position, and agreed to

take the mandatory classes to allow him to begin in that area immediately. When I (EL) called Human Resources, I was told that he was
being sent to the most sought-after magnate high school, a position he
had accepted. Although the Human Resources representative told me
that MVS was never brought up in their conversation, I wondered why
the representative did not even ask Mark about being placed as a
teacher at MVS based on his background and experience; most rea-
sonable professionals would have. This representative could have either
led him toward MVS or away from MVS. Why was the choice to lead
him away? Was the real issue our least-favored status at this central
administration office? This teacher left the state the next year. The
agenda became clear when teacher Annette Perry said to me, "I was
told not to go to 'that' school." She came anyway and stayed.

*Posing a threat to the central office power base, a new innovative
school will be targeted and the resolve of its staff challenged in
ways that reach beyond imagination. However, if you keep
pounding away at good ideas and those ideas are logical and begin
to show success, systemic change will follow.*

With so many teacher vacancies and no one to fill them, creativity
must again dominate the thinking; every resource must be checked and
double-checked to get the teachers needed to make it through the year
and beyond. Every potential educator must be scrutinized, as you never
know where expertise lies.

Substitute teachers filled vacant positions while we hustled for permanent ones. We searched far and wide for a capable foreign-language
teacher, a subject area requested by our parents. Beginning to
improvise, we noticed one of our classroom substitute teachers in
special education was African and spoke Swahili. After a short conversation, Mr. Elijah Mualuko became our long-term substitute foreign-
language teacher, and our foreign language became Swahili. The task
of hiring special education teachers, extremely difficult under normal
circumstances, had us reaching for any caring educator who was sen-
sitive to children with needs. There were simply no special education
teachers available. While inquiring about a posted educational assistant
position, a prospective employee mentioned she had a degree in African

studies. She told us she had spent time with a relative with a disabling condition and expressed interest in continuing toward her certification in special education. After being sent to the University of Wisconsin, Milwaukee, to sign up for classes and to Human Resources to be hired, Ms. Yolanda Tynes turned out to be a hard-working and willing learner. We got lucky, as there were no other choices; almost half of the special education teachers in the Milwaukee public school system were not fully certified. Many positions, throughout the system, were filled by teachers completely unprepared to work with children with special needs, who were taking their first university classes toward certification. Others were filled by long-term substitutes who were not certified at all.

I finally found time to sit down with classroom substitute teacher Meg Skiewrawski. We were talking about her background when she casually mentioned she had a degree in music. MUSIC? MUSIC! MUSIC? Nearly dropping out of my chair, I recovered enough to change her placement, and she was soon ready to go; she did a wonderful job as our new long-term substitute music teacher. "Okay, what's next?" I wondered. "In what back alley will I find the next teacher?" With someone in place in all positions, we began the teaching and team-building process. We let nothing stand in our way.

A small budget with no money to support after-school activities during the first few years had dedicated staff members taking the lead. Tim Fosshage, the school psychologist, volunteered his time to help coach three basketball teams, while social worker Bill Brooks went on field trips and chaperoned a horseback-riding trip. I (MGB) volunteered to run after-school drug-free activities. After school tutoring with teachers Harry Collins, Annette Perry, LaShawn Roscoe, and Catherine (Hnat) Spivey was a mainstay. Eldon took students out for "dinner with the principal" to reward their volunteer work efforts at the school and taught trumpet and trombone. Monique Brown coordinated the Best Friends Program. All volunteered and never asked for a penny.

> *Working together, with everyone doing his or her part, quickly leads to the cost-effective start of a new school. Every human resource is utilized to develop an effective program for students.*

GETTING STARTED

Teamwork, essential to our philosophy, is the toughest concept to develop. Seasoned administrators concur that a staff with experience working together for a long time is the greatest asset to a school. Teamwork, planning, and all the intricacies of running a school are supported by experience, but so is entrenchment. Teachers used to doing the same thing in the same old way become entrenched in old habits that are hard to change. Dramatic change, necessary to a new school, requires that staff members know each other and be able to work together to accept changes fundamental to the philosophy.

The team-building process is slow and methodical, but must be addressed. A natural, but torturous, process, team building entails several stages of development, as described to us by colleagues Chuck Gobel and Derrick Brewer and documented in the B. W. Tuckman article "Developmental Sequence in Small Groups":

1. *Forming*. In this stage, everyone is happy and excited to get the new school started and totally oblivious of reality. Enter the children, and everything soon changes. As they are not used to the new design, the students and staff have no routine to fall back on. Thus, the second stage is conceived.
2. *Storming*. This is the roughest stage in the team-building process, as evidenced by its name. Reality invades the heretofore perfect world as staff members are now less patient with each other. In fact, it can even get downright ugly. Teachers were overheard saying:

   "I need my time. My union contract says I get my free time."
   "You can't tell me what to do."
   "Get your kids in order, I have mine to take care of."
   "Kids need letter grades, that's what parents understand and that's what I'm going to give them."

   During that first year, due to the frustration of a total educational shift, everyone gave up at one time or another. The storming stage may seem to last forever, but eventually the team will move on, only to begin storming again every time new staff are added or crises occurs.

3. *Norming.* Staff members slowly begin to trust each other for the good of the children. At least, they have a better understanding of each other and begin to bond as a unit, paving the way for the final stage.
4. *Performing.* Staff members, now comfortable with the new routine, as well as with each other, become free to be creative.

These are natural stages; some of our teachers went through them successfully, and some didn't. Every time new staff is added, the process starts all over again. Adding a grade level every year for three years, the process will cycle at least three times. Methodical team-building activities, built into the ongoing school plan, provide time for staff members to enjoy and get to know each other in social situations, as well as during the structured activities. Team building, planning, and a steady hand are crucial to the success of a school.

One such team-building activity, the ropes course, utilizes actual ropes in unique ways. One example is a spiderweb of ropes designed between two trees where teachers have to help each other get through this maze without touching the ropes. This requires an enormous amount of teamwork. Of more difficulty are the high elements: a teacher, wearing a harness, walks a tightrope high in the air, while the partner on the ground pulls on a rope to maintain stability. Again, teamwork is essential. Psychologist Tim Fosshage describes the activity:

> The outing at the Milwaukee Public School Ropes and Challenge Course for MVS staff was a daylong event. The ropes course manager and I were responsible for planning the activities designed to provide the Village staff the opportunities and skills to help enhance trust, communication, problem solving, and decision making. The objective was to promote group cooperation and cohesion. The skills that were demonstrated on the rope course can be directly applied to working together as a staff within the school setting. The goal of the day was to help establish trust and promote communication among the staff members, most of whom had just recently met each other. The day consisted of using both cooperative game activities, as well as utilizing the ropes course stations for individual challenges; i.e., climbing up obstacles approximately twenty feet high. Overall, some of the staff members were very apprehensive at

the beginning of the day, but, as the day progressed, some barriers were broken and the first stages of cooperation and honest communication were developed.

The inability to work in a team is a nationwide problem. Whether it's in industry or the business of running a school, overcoming this problem is essential. In education, we have the ability to start with our youngest children. As we teach teamwork constantly throughout the students' school years, the problem will diminish in their adult years.

Recognize the stages of development and provide a continuous flow of team-building activities. This is a constant, conscious effort for staff and students alike.

Diving head first into reform requires the ability to accept the reality of Murphy's law—anything that can go wrong will. To succeed, we must have the tenacity to forge forward, realizing perfection will come only after years of adjustments. This is extremely challenging, as evidenced by the very few who try it, and when the children walk into the building for the first time, everything will start over. In preparation for the first day, a significant amount of planning time is essential. Not only is it necessary to develop team building, it is clearly essential to ensure that all components of a new school are in place. Several months of planning are ideal, but we were content with the two weeks we were allocated. Enter Murphy's law again; the system hiring process was dramatically behind and we were of least-favored status. Short of teachers, we had to make do, not only to refine the curriculum, but also to plan for the first three weeks of school. We developed a partnership with Milwaukee's innovative Alverno College to help us get started. With their help, we developed our first proficiencies, those goals and objectives that drive the Village curriculum. Rolled paper sheets hung all over the walls, and ideas poured out everywhere from the few staff members we had. We accomplished our goals, but most staff members were hired after that session was complete. In fact, most were hired only a day or two before school started, while some came on board after school started. Those teachers were unprepared for their new experience, yet another devastating blow to the start of a new school.

We simply adjusted, as always, and we did it on the run. Not the ideal way to start a school, but if we could make it through the first year, the second year would be better.

To start a new school, staff must be hired well in advance of the student starting date. Plan as much staff development and planning time as you can during the first year, even if it cuts into student time. The issue is quality education, and change takes a constant exchange of ideas.

We could almost hear the students clamoring at the door to get in while newly hired teachers were hastily putting their rooms together at the last minute. Everyone was scrounging for additional tables and chairs and other classroom furnishings, while the secretary was busy assembling partitions for the makeshift offices. Supplies, long delayed by a union strike, had just arrived, containing a shipment of tables essential to every classroom, "assembly needed." With no maintenance people available, we looked to the children for support, and they came through in spectacular fashion. Assembling tables was the order of the day. With drills and screwdrivers in hand, Dan Hamilton, the safety aide, led an assembly team of students, staff, lead administrators, and whoever walked by to achieve that goal. Yes, we did overcome those obstacles for now, and students were the key. It was their school; they helped set it up and continued to help run this school designed for children.

Allow the children to make the school their own. They will help you run it.

CHAPTER 3

Looking at the World in Different Ways

Driven by no. 2 pencils and bubble sheets, today's curriculum has educators chasing their tails, trying to fit all students into a standardized box filled with word games and math riddles. Ill prepared for the challenges of life, today's children are left to the struggle of living day to day in an elitist world. For years we've tinkered with education, only to dig the hole of entrenchment deeper and deeper. The massive effort needed to change the way we educate children will take more energy than one can imagine. Starting where the teacher meets the child, the time has come to truly respect the intelligence and abilities of all children. It's time to let them out of their little boxes.

As they entered MVS for the first time, parents, students, and even teachers were asking, "What's going on?"

"Where are the schedules?" one parent asked. "What classes does my child have?"

"Well, we don't have an eight-period day, so there is no set schedule for classes. Integrated learning does not necessarily go under the label of a class, but it does include all the basics," I (EL) explained.

"If you say so," the puzzled parent said and left.

"We don't have enough social studies books to go around," lamented a teacher.

"Of course not. They are resources, not a curriculum in this school," I said.

"I can't teach unless I have the *Basic One Science Book*," said another.

"We don't have that one. We don't follow the textbook as our curriculum," we said.

But how are the kids going to learn? We start by putting children in a leadership role. Leadership, a quality not often taught in schools, will help develop a community within the school that will drive it for years to come. In the words of authors Gary Goldman and Jay Newman in *Empowering Students to Transform Schools*:

> Schools, even low achieving ones, can change positively and dramatically as they create a community in which the goal is not to do something to students but for students to become productive workers and leaders. When such a cultural change is undertaken, the school becomes a significant force in moving the community to higher levels of decency and humanity. (p. 7)

How do we create student leaders and get them aboard to buy into our journey? We believe hands-on leadership training is the direction to take. Let's get our children to accept the concept that they have some control over their educational lives. Let's set a tone of putting the children in the leadership seat long before school starts.

I (MGB) suggested horseback riding. I knew of a horse ranch forty-five minutes away in the rural, rolling hills of Southern Wisconsin's Kettle Moraine area, totally foreign to the inner-city experiences of many of our children. A former student of mine, Al Gagliano, along with his wife, Cindy, not only ran the Kettle Moraine Ranch, but was also wonderful with kids. Al's powerful way of mingling education with the challenges of horseback riding was bred from his personal experience: quitting school, running a gang in Chicago, and getting his eye shot out were all part of his life before I met him on his return to high school. Al's remarkable return to school has made a memorable impression on me, and there he was, a learning resource and role model for our new student leaders. The first twenty students to sign up for MVS were our riding candidates. With parental permission obtained, the MVS leadership philosophy was set in motion a month before school was to start. Students Chante, April, and Prince ventured into the nonthreatening learning challenges of a whole new world in rural Kettle Moraine. Donning our hiking boots, school social worker Bill Brooks, psychologist Tim Fosshage, and I dreamed that this frontier moment would culminate in our children leading the village and changing their community. Only time would make our dreams for them come true!

The horseback-riding experience was a metaphor of our dreams for the children and the future of the Village. The strong, confident experience of the horses guided us through the countryside, just as we hoped these future student leaders would fearlessly guide their peers through the journey of a new school-community experience. In the pleasant setting of the ranch, we could talk, we could laugh, we could understand each other; now as educators, we could mold the future leaders of our school. Yes, these children would later share the joy of this day with their new classmates, and yes, these children would indeed prove to be our school leaders for the next three years. A simple, pleasant, bonding experience in the rural countryside went a long way to building a student-centered school.

The need to continue this bonding process was evident. Planned as a yearly event, overnight camping trips helped to develop a co-dependency in a foreign environment that brought our children together as a team. Clearly a goal of management in most occupations is to help people work together, supporting each other for the betterment of the whole. In a rural setting deep in the woods, students become the leaders, planning together, working together, playing together, and depending on each other in close quarters. What a phenomenal team-building experience away from urban clutter where the sounds are few and the stars are bright; where a simple walk through the woods brings out stories of history, mythology, zoology, and botany and provides a whole range of learning experiences; where imaginations wander to speculate as to what abominable critter is peering from behind the tree deep in the woods.

The students, nervous with anticipation, prepared to leave on a late-night walk through the woods. Silly playing turned to silence as the "snipe" was described and our effort to catch this elusive critter planned. Slowly we crept into the woods following what they didn't know was a predetermined path designed to allow for the enjoyment of the sights and sounds of nature. The sound of rustling bushes had wide-eyed children wondering, What is it? Who is it following? Leading the pack of adventure seekers, I (EL) was quick to point out what appeared to be a nest of branches, a clear sign that snipe were nearby. A hush came over the crew as another rustling had this school leader, credibility in danger, diving headfirst into the nest, struggling with the largest of all snipe. As I called for assistance, only Sean came stumbling through the darkness to help as the rest looked on in anticipation. "I'm coming, I'm coming, Mr. Lee. I see it! I see its eyes!" hollered Sean as he tripped over some branches and rolled in my direction. Mysteriously, the snipe escaped just before he got there, leaving only a pile of leaves, but the sight of their administrator, covered head to toe in mud, gave the students a different view of their fearless leader.

Teachers, children, and parents were all seen as people first. Teachers, still the disciplinarians and sources to be reckoned with, became stronger role models, as they were seen in a relaxed atmosphere. Teacher LaShawn Roscoe said, "If you are willing to put your 'all' into it and if you let go of those problems due to what the teacher relationship is 'spozed' to be . . . and break through and get to a humanistic quality . . . that's when the educational opportunity is seized upon."

As we continued our walk through the woods, we pointed out vegetation, as well as animal tracks and sounds. A look to the sky through a clearing saw the comet Hale-Bopp making its way to a new destination. We paused in an opening at the end of the trail to have a discussion about constellations not clearly visible in the city and the mythology behind those forms in the sky. The Big Dipper pointed to the Little Dipper and the North Star; a discussion of the Underground Railroad led to the words of the song "Follow the Drinking Gourd." What wonderful teachable moments!

Safely back in camp, the lights were turned off, and the students crawled into bed. As they listened to a late-night scary story, the room became silent. Who would be the next to fall victim to the ghost of Bloody Stubby, the ghost that haunts these grounds looking for victims? It was almost too quiet in the cabin. Had the children fallen asleep already? We turned on the lights to find eight of the toughest eleven-year-old boys you've ever seen, scared silly, all hiding in one bed, being the children they were allowed to be here. We often referred to them affectionately as our "babies," as we clearly recognized what was under their tough exterior, an experience all educators should have. Coupled with environmental instruction throughout the day, the camping trip led to twenty-four-hour learning with barely enough time to sleep. Not one child complained. We were all scared together, excited together, laughing together, and bonding in an atmosphere far from the daily routine. What better way to bring these eleven-year-old children together as a team?

> *Student team building should begin before the first day of school. Student leaders, taking charge of their own lives, can be a most powerful school resource.*

DOING THE RIGHT THING

As visitors walked through the front door of MVS, a wall of photos immediately caught their eye. The photos, featuring students, parents, and teachers involved in positive activities, were selected at random, enlarged to 11" × 17" and rotated, with all students eventually taking their rightful place in the spotlight.

It is always a thrill to see the smiles light up on the faces when students realize it is "me" on that wall. But shouldn't the spotlight be reserved for the winners, the best of the best? Feeling good about doing good things is not limited to the winner of a contest. We aren't interested in just the geniuses. Our school philosophy is designed for all children, and all children do good things. When children do good things, they get recognized. Can you imagine how many children's good deeds are ignored, when only the winner is acknowledged? The focus of the Village philosophy is on the individual gains of all students, not the massive "raking a few geniuses" concept from the day of Thomas Jefferson. We want all students to develop the skills, abilities, and character to have a good and productive life.

BUILDING CHARACTER

A part of everyday life, character building is essential to a child's education. As a matter of fact, few people are fired from their jobs for lack of skills; usually it's due to work-related behaviors. You mean we should teach values in a public school? Of course we should. The value of respect as demonstrated through skills as simple as saying please and thank you can be helpful in life, as can the more complex skill of understanding the feelings of others. Also considered are safety skills, such as what to do when a stranger is following you home, as well as good manners like asking permission. With a wide range of skills needed, it is difficult to determine which ones to focus on. Again, we look to the teachers along with the parents to pick the skills most needed. A survey of all parents lists a whole range of character-building skills that might be of value to their children. This information is put in rank order and used as a strong guideline by teachers as they get together to develop the curriculum. Like most effective curriculums, ours is flexible, and the process is revisited every year. A skill of the week was selected to reinforce positive values constantly. Here is how our character-building program was designed:

- Skills to be presented were determined from parent and teacher surveys.
- Teachers then set up a Skill of the Week schedule.
- All skills could be increased beyond a week if needed.
- Skills were reinforced weekly with banners hung at various locations around the school as a constant reminder.
- We designed cards, called M&M RAP by the staff at Bell Middle School, Milwaukee Public Schools, meaning Manners Matter, Respect All People.
  - Not rewards for learning, these cards were simply constant reminders of good manners.
  - All staff were stocked with M&M RAP cards to give out to students who had utilized a specific skill.
  - Students turned in the cards they had received for displaying the skill, and a drawing was held for various incentives, such as a healthy treat from the school store.
  - This process was reversed occasionally, with the students giving the cards to staff members when they remembered to say please and thank you.

Germaine approached me (EL) in the hall and said out of the blue, "Thank you, Mr. Lee."

"Thank you for what, Germaine?" I asked.

"Just thank you," he said as he glanced down at my hand full of M&M RAP cards.

"Pleeeeeeeeze Germaine, that's a nice try but you must be thanking someone for something to get a card," I said.

"Oh! Ummm, okay, thank you for being you!" exclaimed Germaine.

"Okay, okay, okay, you get a card," I sighed.

What is important is that we set their minds moving toward the use of polite words. The more students say them, the more they use them. It is great fun, as well as a daily reminder that good character is an essential quality. Teachers must also make a point of modeling the skill. Hmmmm. What a thought, all teachers saying please and thank you to students. It was really interesting to reverse the process. Students had cards to give the teachers when they utilized the skill. Do all the teachers in your school say please and thank you? Are we, as educators, good role models for student character?

The M&M RAP cards are effective with simple skills, but how do we approach the more complex skills? What about the skill of using self-control? This is a difficult area for those children of middle school age. We make no claim that character-building activities will solve all problems; but these exercises do give students some strategies necessary to get them out of compromising situations.

My (MGB's) dog-eared, ragtag, semibible of Goldstein et al.'s book entitled *Skillstreaming the Adolescent*, which I piloted for the University of Wisconsin, Milwaukee, back in 1980, became the backbone for our teaching of character development. Included in this book are step-by-step suggestions to walk the students through the process. Consider the four steps used to support the skill of using self-control.

1. Tune in to what is going on in your body. That helps you know when you are about to lose control of yourself.
2. Decide what happened to make you feel this way.
3. Think about ways you might control yourself.
4. Choose the best way to control yourself, and do it.

With these steps in mind, proceed to develop good character in the classroom on a daily basis.

- Introduce the skill to the child.
  — Ask the students how and under what conditions this skill can be used.
  — Discuss the steps to achieving success in the skill area.
  — Have students write the skill information in their notebook for future reference.
- Revisit the skill.
  — Highlight key words in the steps to achieving success in the skill area.
  — Place banners throughout the school identifying the skill area.
  — Review when to use the skill.
- Have students write a role-play.
  — Have students write a short play in small groups using a situation that calls for the skill.
  — The students in the small groups decide what parts each will play. Included are the director, cameraperson, and actors.
- Practice the role-play.
  — This is simply rehearsal time; everyone assumes her or his role.
  — This may be video taped for the purpose of review.
- Perform the role-play.
  — Students perform in front of their own class first, and then proceed to other classes.
  — Videotape the final product for presentation throughout the years.

Their play unfolds:
Four students, Angela, Mary, John, and Rodney, are sitting at the table working. Rodney throws a paper wad and hits Angela in the face.
Mary: Why did you do that, John?
Angela: (standing up) Yeah, John, why did you do that?
John: (standing up) Man, I didn't do that!
Angela: (pushing John) Don't be getting loud with me. You did it!
John: (pushing back, then pointing at Rodney) I didn't do it. He did it!
They both sit down.
Rodney: (talking to John and laughing) That was funny.
John: (to Rodney, getting more angry) You got everyone mad at me.
Rodney: (to John and Angela) Oh, I'm sorry, I did it.

Angela: (to John) I'm sorry, I should have thought about it before I got mad at you. I should have controlled my temper.

John, who had difficulty with anger management in the past, was either the best actor I had ever seen or he was really getting angry when Angela pushed him. This lesson was well worth presenting. The role-plays were great, but of equal importance was the connection made with the home. Send a processing sheet home for both parent and child to follow through on. Here is one sample from the first week MVS was in existence:

9/11/95

Dear parent of Quincy Rogers

This week we are learning about the social communication skill:
Listening

This social skill is very important to interpersonal relationships.
This skill can be broken down into the following areas. Please watch for all these steps in your play or real-life observation:

- Look at the person who is talking.
- Think about what is being said.
- Wait your turn to talk.
- Say what you want to say.

Please complete one of the following activities with your son or daughter. Put an X by your choice.

_____   A. We acted out the role-play situation listed.

___X___   B. I observed my son/daughter using this skill in a real-life situation.

Description of real-life situation: We were watching TV, and I asked Quincy a question about the show. He answered the question too fast. He didn't think about what was asked. He waited after the fact and said what he had to say. After we talked about what was asked, he understood what was asked of him. Quincy has one problem. He answers a question before the question is asked.

Student listens to parent as directions are given.

Please underline the word below which best describes how your son/daughter did while using the social skill.

Needs More Help   (Good)   **Excellent**

But needs to take his time and think about the question.

It is important for you to reinforce your child's use of social skills at home in a positive way.

Thank you for your assistance.

Parent signature: _____*Vernay Rogers*_____

> *Character building is, at the very least, a constant reminder to students about simple social skills. Often, through role-playing, a needed skill can be developed.*

Sometimes the role-plays are as simple as that discussed above with these eleven-year-olds. Sometimes they can turn into a complete story. Again, this is no cure-all for school problems. At the very least, it brings the skills to the attention of students in many different ways. At the very most, some might recognize or even internalize a skill, helping them overcome a crisis situation. As a bonus, students refine their reading, writing, and speaking skills in yet another way.

WHAT DID YOU LEARN IN SCHOOL TODAY? DOES ANYONE KNOW?

A question parents often ask students when they arrive home after a long day at school is, What did you learn in school today? The response is often a less-than-enthusiastic "I dunno." In today's world of standardized tests and less-than-accurate letter grades, it remains uncertain whether anyone knows what is learned on a daily basis. There is even some question whether teachers can focus on what children learn on a given day. We know they got 78 percent on the chapter test. We know they turned in 86 percent of their homework. We know they attended 94 percent of the time. But the question remains, What did you learn in school today? Absolutely essential to the Village philosophy is a strong focus that requires student involvement in a daily routine that reminds them, and their teachers, what they are going to learn and what they have learned. The process starts with goal setting every morning.

- Daily goal setting
  — Making the statement. "This is what we are going to do today." really sets the stage for learning. Students address this every morning.
  — Growth charts make a great visual aid to keep students focused.
  — Daily tasks, documented by students in specially designed assignment notebooks, have check-off spaces for student self-evaluation at the end of each day. Together, teacher and students transform a general assignment into workable goals, such as these samples:
    – Communications.
    – Language: Write three paragraphs for "Who Am I?" books.
    – Reading: Introduce a new book, explain a folktale, and list the vocabulary words.
    – Problem solving/analytical thinking
    – Computing: Determine the degree of an angle.
- Community awareness
  — Community resources: Begin mapping the neighborhood to understand mapping concepts.
- Professional preparation:
  — Skill of the week is understanding the feelings of others.
  — Develop a role-play and choose a character to play.

Although education is presented through integrated projects and community experiences, the goals and student focus must also remain in academic areas; progress in fundamental areas is essential to the child's development.

Now that we have a focus on daily goals, what about long-term goals? How do we address that issue? We address it in the same way we do the daily goals, but of course, not so often.

Yearly, long-range goals and action plans are developed.

- I will improve my attendance by 5 percent. My action plan is:
  — Get an alarm clock.
  — Tell friends I won't skip school with them.
  — Go to bed by 10 P.M.
- I will gain knowledge of chemistry as a future profession. My action plan is:
  — Visit a chemist on the job.
  — Become familiar with the quadratic equation and other needed math.
  — Do a chemistry-related project for the science fair.

Plans are revised and rewritten as new ideas and thoughts are explored. Group discussions with guest speakers are held on a regular basis to reinforce daily and yearly goals. Occasionally, these groups are divided by gender to discuss issues such as menstruation, sexuality, sexually transmitted diseases, and related issues, where the comfort level allows a free and open discussion. Guest speakers rotate from one small group to another, motivating the children to think about their future.

What better way to end a day at school than by having students voice their opinions and simply talk about "what I learned today." Wrap-up sessions at the end of every school day are used to process what was accomplished throughout the day. This is primarily a self-evaluation for the students with assistance from the teacher. Initially, students review the objectives that they set up first thing in the morning and proceed to their growth charts to celebrate their progress. We use visible growth charts, indicating projects that are to be completed or readings to be done. These objectives are like the daily to-do list or grocery list, constantly maintained by adding and crossing off tasks or purchases. Students respond to how many they can cross off their to-do list for that day. This information is individually documented in their assignment notebooks. The objectives they did not accomplish are set up as goals for the next day. Rarely do more than one or two students miss the same objectives on a given day. This is a clear indicator that children progress at different rates and in different ways. The assignment notebooks are shared with parents on a regular basis. Now when parents ask, "What did you learn in school today?" these charts and assignment notebooks can be shared with them. They can see if their child is or is not completing assignments and progressing. They are a vivid reminder if a child was absent and did not make up work! They actually speak louder than words! Students make regular visits to the growth charts on the wall to monitor their own progress. This opens pathways of conversation between parent and child, allowing yet another chance for them to work together.

A daily performance self-evaluation goes home weekly to keep parents aware of their child's effort.

Daily Performance Report
Self-Evaluation
Key:
5 = Excellent performance
4 = Good performance
3 = Average performance
2 = Needs some improvement
1 = Needs much improvement

I will be able to:	Day 1	Day 2	Day 3	Day 4	Day 5	Total	Average
1. Have proper materials	___	___	___	___	___	___	___
2. Cooperate with adults	___	___	___	___	___	___	___
3. Use positive language	___	___	___	___	___	___	___
4. Show positive interaction	___	___	___	___	___	___	___
5. Finish projects on time	___	___	___	___	___	___	___
6. Use unstructured time well	___	___	___	___	___	___	___
7. Cooperate in group situations	___	___	___	___	___	___	___
8. Work to the best of my ability	___	___	___	___	___	___	___

Parents, note which skills your son or daughter must practice. Please sign and return.

Parent signature _____ Date _____
Phone _____

The strong character necessary for success becomes inherent in students who keep a strong focus throughout the year.

TAKING CHILDREN FROM WHERE THEY ARE

By refusing to lump all children into one tiny robotic mold, we proceed to develop a plan to reach all children and meet them where they are.

Crucial to our philosophy is recognizing that children learn at different rates and in many different ways: from their own research, from each other, from the community, from technology, from groups, or from themselves. They have so many things to learn. To begin this educational adventure, we must determine, in a realistic way, where students are in the learning process and how to continue. For our initial assessment, we used the Brigance Comprehensive Inventory of Basic Skills. What makes this different from the usual standardized test? It is designed to give information to teachers simply for the purpose of a baseline to get children started on a personalized learning mission. Another difference is that it is given individually and not used to judge, but simply as a starting point. We were determined to prove that teaching and assessing the whole person makes a more significant difference. It was our primary focus. With this in mind, we begin our journey:

- Develop a baseline using the Brigance or a similar assessment for math, graphing, sentence structure, and spelling (simply used as a baseline).
- Apply personal attention for oral vocabulary, oral reading, and comprehensive reading.
  — Apply one-on-one attention to understand fully the child's true ability to read. This can be done even in a large school, with a team of assessors.
  — Document information that will help develop a lesson plan centered on the child's true skills.

Quite frankly, assessment, or more accurately, ongoing demonstrations of learning, are a critical component of the philosophy. They are more than a map of the child's knowledge; they are the stepping-stones for the child's entire learning experience. It should not be cheapened with the narrow scope and convenience of the standardized multiple-choice test. Author John Merrow sees this testing as a "mad (and doomed) rush to find a single measure of school and student quality" (p. 3), without regard for the students gifted in art or those needing more time on engineering projects. Life and learning are problem-solving experiences, not multiple-choice tests. Yet far too often these false prophets of assessment are applied to track students into failure-filled lives. The joy and thrill of learning is squelched for the convenience of placing some children into an endless flow of failure. Think about it. Where has this standardized form of testing led us?

Assessment, by contrast, is an essential wave in the ongoing flow of learning. It is not an irrelevant map of student reaction to multiple-choice options. Rather, it is an indicator of the child as a problem solver, as a human being, as an individual learner. Information is for educators, helping them to plan for student progress, not for politicians hiding behind radio microphones. With our philosophy, portfolio assessment and self-assessment are perfect fits for these criteria. What do we actually mean by "portfolio"? A portfolio is a collection of student work showing the student's accomplishments and allowing the student to recognize his or her gains.

Maintaining a portfolio keeps the student focused, and a focused student is a powerful learner.

- Portfolios, of course, are varied with a multiple-intelligence per-spective that displays a variety of the child's possibilities.
- Portfolios may feature pictures, videotapes, written work, and project samples; the list of possibilities is endless.

After all, who could imagine Steven Spielberg not being allowed to have visual materials as a part of his portfolio? Limiting the portfolio potential of our students is, in effect, limiting the future genius of our society. Inherent to the portfolio is self-assessment. Children update and create their academic identity through portfolio creation. Such a process involves self-reflection, which is indicative of higher-order critical thinking. A student demonstrating an awareness of his or her own growth is a key element of the learning process. After all, don't important problem solvers like Spielberg thrive on the process of self-assessment before they take their next step on the journey of creativity?

Cumbersome in the eyes of those who support mass production, the Portfolio Proof of Learning takes a lot of work, for teachers and students alike. As children grow, their portfolios grow. The portfolios embody their decisions, as they add to them, change them, and replace old items with the new.

The portfolio is more than assessment; it in fact becomes the story of the child's educational life, and it is passed from one grade to the next, as well as one school to the next. Imagine, real information available to a student's new school. A great way to start!

The following lists items that might be found in an academic portfolio:

- Assessment information (remains until the next assessment for the purpose of comparison)
  — Proficiency checklist (documentation of skills achieved)
  — Fall and spring reading assessment
  — Formal math assessment
  — Sentence-writing assessment
  — Personal letter with envelope, fully addressed
- Actual daily projects (students constantly replace the contents while keeping the previous project to show growth)
- Communication skills
  — Writing samples
  — Examples of artistic expression
  — Video or audio tape with a speaking or singing samples
- Problem solving and analytical thinking
  — Sample of math used in a project
  — Sample of science used in a project
- Community awareness
  — Self-evaluation of a community experience
  — Sample of project
  — Personal evaluation of a visit

Assessment is the lifeblood of learning. It must be a continuous process, built into the daily routine. It is a tool to reach our most important goal: to hold on to every child!

Students, taking command of their academic direction through portfolios, growth charts, and other means, develop the focus needed to learn. After all, we are not here to throw out education for students to catch in a bushel basket; rather, they ask for it, and we help them get it.

Put in charge of their destinies, students have focus, choose priorities, and drive the active engine of learning. When learning is active, it becomes fun; it becomes real to the students who take charge of their own destiny. Active learners, in charge of their lives, will break the barriers of the teachers' goals. Why stop the explosion of growth to surmise irrelevant multiple-choice options? And then, consider the other world of so-called learning where students sit silently, passively absorbing the lectures of talking heads, the world where students are forced to give up recess or the arts, just to memorize trivial data for a multiple-choice test—information that is forgotten shortly afterward. Remember, children can memorize when forced to; they only learn when they decide to. They control their minds. Students learn better when they have the perception and the reality that the information is meaningful to them.

Armed with real data, teachers march forward together with children, enriching lives. Students learn in unforeseen ways, in ways the bubble tests cannot measure. Teachers unleash their creative juices when they are free to teach academic lessons in a variety of ways and locations. Why limit learning to the classroom? After all, a sound philosophy requires a generalization of lessons outside the borders of the classroom. Hands-on experiences are required for learning and, quite frankly, assessment without hands-on observation is heresy.

An important part of taking the children from where they are is for everyone to understand where he or she is going. A curriculum guide in the form of a proficiency checklist should be drawn up by teachers and parents each year to ensure that children are learning what is valuable to them and of interest to their parents. The checklist must focus on the fundamentals of reading, writing, speaking, mathematics, science, research, and other elements necessary to everyday life. It does not need to come from a central administration or a state or federal bureaucracy. It comes from the neighborhood, using state and other standards as guidelines.

A proficiency checklist, updated every year, serves as a general curriculum guide.

- A one-number rubric is used to determine mastery. Terms like "progressing" and "needs improvement" are irrelevant. As the old saying goes, close only counts in horseshoes and hand grenades. Our students either are A students or are going to be A students. There are no other options.

- Attempts at mastery are documented on the checklist, along with statements regarding student needs.
- Proficiencies in the fundamental academic areas of study must be documented to maintain the focus.
- Proficiencies are not one or two questions or projects given at the end of the year. They are a wide range of demonstrations of learning that can be mastered anytime.

The first proficiency checklist at MVS was nine pages long. These demonstrations of learning could be suited to individual student needs.

> *Let's stop labeling children and holding them hostage to the convenience of standardized tests. None of our children are without talents to assess and nurture, so let's get down to business and build assessment into learning.*

TURNING TEACHERS LOOSE

When not controlled by textbooks or preprinted curriculums, educators seek other resources for educational direction. Since themes are general in nature, they become a valuable tool, as they help educators focus on student needs when developing their units. These themes vary in length depending on the needs of the lesson. Under this process, educators are allowed the flexibility and creativity and given the drive to accomplish wonders. As teachers get together, they take charge of their educational lives by teaming to develop these themes. Starting by brainstorming, all ideas are welcomed and publicly recorded in an effort to develop the themes. The following is a simple process to bring all thoughts together:

- Staff members meet in small groups to develop and exchange thematic ideas.
- Small-group consensus is reached and chosen ideas are listed.

- Together, as a complete staff, these ideas are shared and recorded for all to see.
- Similar ideas are combined.
  — Which ones fit together?
  — What projects and what academic achievements can be accomplished under a given theme. Discussions would be, "Under this theme we can do . . ."
- The list is whittled down to the necessary number of themes.

This is really nothing new. What is creative is that the staff then determines the number of weeks necessary to complete each theme without regard to six-week, nine-week, or other limited time frames. Thinking within these time frames is a difficult habit to break, and even the staff at MVS had difficulty doing it. Teachers must be allowed the flexibility to meet and plan, changing learning units from three weeks to four weeks to six weeks in length, depending on the themes. They must use this freedom to determine where students are placed on a daily basis. After all, teachers are the ones who are doing the assessment; therefore, they are the ones adjusting the time frames so that assessment is driven by the project and by the students' needs, rather than the other way around. What a method to bring focus to the implementation of lessons! Teachers become creative teachers, who build creative students, who break learning boundaries.

Identity was chosen for our initial theme at MVS, and the first class eagerly began a quest for the school's nickname and mascot. Those first students defined the school through their own eyes. To accomplish their important task, students needed to learn diplomacy, negotiation skills, compromise strategies, and interpersonal communication techniques. They felt this was their school, and they were creating the permanent identity of a school that would forever be the icon of their neighborhood. Should we have stopped the process to determine whether the learned interpersonal skills were integrated into a standardized bubble test? By setting our children off on a real-world, group problem-solving task, we were not labeling them on the basis of standards. Instead, we were creating a mind-set for something much more important.

"Who's in the Bag?" is a project designed to help students under-stand their identities as well as the identities of others. Lorna Hockett, a teacher at Waldport Elementary School, developed this project. This team-building/introductory activity fits well into the identity theme, especially at the beginning of the year. Here students tell something about themselves to other students through items brought from home.

- Objectives
    — Introduce students to each other and the school staff.
    — Improve students' reading and writing skills.
    — Determine mathematical averages.
    — Demonstrate the importance and use of charting.
    — Practice techniques of research.
    — Discuss the conservation of woodlands.
- Materials
    — Each student brings a shopping bag and personal items.
- Activities
    — Students bring three or four personal items to school in a shopping bag. Students are directed to bring items that will tell others something about themselves.
    — The teacher empties the bags, one at a time, in front of the class.
    — Students discuss the content of the bag before guessing the owner.
        – What activities does this person enjoy?
        – Why do you think the items were chosen?
        – What item in the bag is the owner especially proud of?
        – Who do you think brought this bag?
- Spin-off activities
    — Write a brief story about the owner based on the information in the bag.
    — Have the owner make a presentation to the class about his or her interests related to items in the bag.
    — Research a unique item from a bag to get detailed information.
    — Determine the average number and chart the items brought by students.
    — Initiate a discussion about the benefits of paper versus plastic bags.

The process of self-identification is especially important for urban children at a neighborhood school. Is there cognitive value here? Of course, as the child's process of selecting limited treasures from a large universe of data at home is not unlike the mission of the archaeologist. Fundamental academic learning fits in everywhere in a natural way. On a project like this, students can do much more writing than in a writing book, and they won't even complain.

THE JOY OF WRITING

Built into the daily routine at MVS, journaling was designed to promote the joy of writing, as well as to provide a forum for expression. These diaries allowed students the freedom to express their individual hopes and dreams, as well as to purge their inner doubts and fears. Prompted by the teacher, students proceeded to write. Even though they were aware the teacher read the journals, the students remained open in their writing. Upon review, the teachers made notes in the margins, but these were not projects that were to be corrected. Students were allowed to express themselves freely without the fear of a grade.

And they did. We read things they would never have told us. B.J. wrote, "Mr. Collins really help me a lot today. That was real nice." However, Selena wrote, "Tony make me mad, I hate him. He touched me in my privates." Selena was a quiet girl and showed little emotion. Upon reading this, our investigation found that the statement was a projection of other compelling problems we were readily able to address. Their hopes and fears came out, and they wrote and wrote and wrote.

Writing is an essential skill and must be practiced every day, everywhere, both inside and outside of school. A review of the rules of writing, however, finds them constantly broken by highly paid authors. Wouldn't it stand to reason that those who utilize the written word set the standard, rather than those who publish textbooks? Bending the rules occasionally, we proceed to instill the joy of writing. Students learn not in the writing class, in dull drab classrooms, not from standardized writing books; nor do they sit in rows and all write the same thing at the same time in the same way. Writing is part of the overall school experience. Every community experience has them writing their plans, taking notes, and writing thank-you letters to those they visited. Projects have them writing more plans, as well as writing reports on their accomplishments. Research has them documenting and presenting information, including the culminating paper. Daily writing is built in everywhere possible.

Promoting writing throughout an extended period of time was the goal of MVS. It was extremely important to cover subject matter that was of interest to students and held their attention. Of course, what do students know better than the story of themselves? Projects like the "Who Am I?" book provide a natural way to improve the following skills. Not only do students write about a subject they know, they are able to take pride in their accomplishments and their growth and the family they come from.

The "Who Am I?" book project simply has students write a book about themselves.

- Objectives
  — Improve students' writing skills.
  — Explore language arts in a creative way.
  — Enhance students' self-concept.
  — Approach diversity.
- Book cover
  — Students design cover artwork with help from an art specialist.
  — The student chooses the title. It must have something to do with "me."
  — The author, of course, is the student.
- Content
  — Chapter 1: Family History
    – The student provides birth date, time, and place.
    – The student provides a family tree.
    – The student conducts family interviews for information.
  — Chapter 2: The Early Years
    – A student interview of family members determines first words, first walking experience, teething, and so forth.
  — Chapter 3: First School Experience
    – A student interview of family, friends, and former teachers provides this information.

— Chapter 4: Attitudes, Hobbies, and Interests
  – A checklist developed by teachers provides suggestions.
  – The student's own information is recalled.
— Chapter 5: Student Character
  – A checklist developed by teachers provides suggestions.
  – The student's own information is recalled.
— Chapter 6: Student's Yearly Goals
  – Goals for in and out of school are described.
  – Information from goal-setting sessions throughout the year is documented.
— Chapter 7: Future Plans and Goals
  – What does the student want to be doing ten years from this date?
  – Student refers to information from goal-setting sessions throughout the year.
• A parent letter is sent fully explaining the project.
  — Home project information to be gathered for Chapter 1.
  — Students will interview parents and other family members.
  — Information from interviews will be written in sentences and paragraphs in class.
  — Correct grammar, punctuation, and writing skills are taught.
  — The information will be written and rewritten before the final product is complete.
  — Additional chapters will be written about activities and academic projects throughout the year.

Interview sheets are provided for student support as per this sample:

Interview sheet for chapter 2: The Early Years.

1. When did I start to walk?
2. When did I start getting teeth?
3. What were my first words?
4. What were my favorite foods?
5. What were my favorite toys?
6. Is there other information that needs to be added?

This is just one of many potential creative projects that have children doing a huge amount of writing. The usual middle school student complaints are not heard as the joy of learning prevails.

When students enjoy writing, they will write constantly, express themselves better, and become better prepared for jobs that require college preparation.

THE THREE Rs: READING, READING, AND MORE READING

Many urban students enter middle school significantly lacking in reading skills, but traditional methods of teaching, such as reading aloud to large classes, clearly aren't working. Quite frankly, having one student read out loud while thirty follow in their books is a highly ineffective way of teaching.

I (EL) had the opportunity to observe such a situation and analyze the results. There were thirty students in the class, and the teacher had good control over the students. All were silent. I timed each student while he or she was reading and charted the eye movements of the remaining students. The results revealed students were actually reading for less than two minutes a day, while over 80 percent of the rest of them had eyes wandering everywhere but on the book. It didn't take a genius to figure out we had to do something different.

It is time to develop a specialized reading program. Begin by bringing the daily routine to a screeching halt for forty-five minutes two times per week. During this time, every adult in the building is put to work helping a group of children practice reading. "Every adult" means every adult and includes the educators, parents, social workers, volunteers, and anyone else who will commit for those times. Reading clubs encourage the joy of reading, and students are supported by the small groups necessary for success.

At MVS, each student was individually assessed using the Brigance Comprehensive Inventory of Basic Skills to arrive at a baseline reading level. My (MGB's) friend, Albert Brigance, a most wonderful, caring gentleman, designed his materials to enable a classroom teacher to assess baselines in a quick, positive way and provide a wealth of feedback to teachers.

The results from the Brigance assessment make clear that children learn at different rates and that in no class are every child's reading skills the same. Students simply are not on the same page in the same text at the same time. After all the research about developmental stages, educators continue to lump everyone into one group based on his or her specific grade. It is ludicrous to think that all students should receive that one basal reader on the first day of school and keep up with the whole class at all times. On the other hand, some students are forced to progress slowly so as to not get too far ahead. Educators need to recognize that the joy of reading doesn't come from a dull, drab basal reader. From the snapshot information given by the assessment, reading groups at MVS were created. Forming the basis of the groups, reading clubs helped students become comfortable with the fact that, within their groups, they all had similar reading abilities, and no one was embarrassed. Consisting of only six or seven students, the beginning readers club was facilitated by two adults. We designed smaller groups for those students who need more intensive reading direction, while the highest-level group had as many as twenty to thirty students in it. All students in the higher-level club came prepared for in-depth group discussions of their reading. Interacting via thought-provoking stories incorporated reading, writing, oral communication, and critical-thinking skills into the sessions to ensure that all students were challenged.

We made enjoyable stories the order of the day, some that students could immediately relate to, and others that allowed them to stretch their imaginations to the heavens and beyond. Various materials and appropriate articles chosen by students were utilized. The goal was to hook students and get them excited about reading, so they will never stop.

At MVS, successes at every level were noted. We used the Caught Reading series, as well as the Be a Better Reader series, from the Globe Feron Company. These had well-disguised grade levels to ensure confidentiality and that students were improving one step at a time. At other times students chose their own books.

Among the readers, Sunny, a new student to our school, showed absolutely no desire to join the group.

"Aw, come and join the group, Sunny," said teacher Ms. Black. "It's fun."

"I can read," replied Sunny. "I don't need help."

"Why don't you come with me? I'll work with you alone for a while," stated teacher Mr. Jabir.

"I'll come, but I ain't doin' no damn reading. I told you, I already know how to read."

This went on for several weeks, and then Sunny finally sat down and tried a word or two, secluded with Mr. Jabir. The strong support and kind words of Mr. Jabir let Sunny know that he was accepted for who he was, and it didn't matter that he was reading at the preprimer level. Three weeks later, Sunny was an active member of his level reading club, reading along with everyone. Whenever he saw Mr. Jabir in the hall, he hollered out, "When are we going to get to read again?" He was improving constantly in reading, but of most significance was that he got the joy of reading. Learning became unstoppable.

Every adult got involved in the reading clubs at MVS. This brought the group size down and made it more personal for the students. Yes, even I (EL), forcing myself to abandon the rigors of principaling, took a journey with nine students consumed by the joy of learning. The short story, from the Be a Better Reader series, was about Admiral Peary's expedition to the North Pole. At his side was African American explorer and close friend Matthew Henson. The story was intriguing, describing the bitter cold as these two explorers, along with four Inuit Eskimos, were the only ones to finally make it to their destination. It was a wonderful experience, and I was right on top of it. I prepared the questions and researched related information. Boy, was I ready to go. No sooner had the group started than I was called to resolve an administrative-type problem that couldn't wait. As I rushed off to the waiting leaky toilet, I told the students to continue reading. Expecting chaos and a significant amount of wasted time, I returned to find, to my amazement, one student reading and the other eight actually following with their eyes. A student, stumbling on a word, gained immediate help from the others, with Carolyn McGee taking the lead. This twelve-year-old allocated sufficient reading time for all and ensured that students would receive help when needed. Carolyn controlled the group with the skill of a seasoned teacher, and when one child started interrupting, a quick stare was all it took. Yep, this administrator knew how to run a good reading group all right: Sit down, shut up, and leave often.

A spin-off activity from the reading groups challenges the highest-level readers to intelligent oral discussions about their readings. Giving twenty to thirty middle school students the opportunity to sit in a circle, draw inferences, analyze characters, organize details, and share critical-thinking skills is totally refreshing.

The fundamental philosophy of MVS was to take students into the community as often as possible, to make learning real. It soon became time to take our show on the road. The idea of a cultural exchange was being considered, so we decided to combine that concept with our high-level reading club to enhance the students' reading experiences. New to my (MGB's) people collection was the assistant superintendent of curriculum for the Beloit, Wisconsin, School District, William Beckley. Located a healthy seventy-five miles down the road, his school was in a much smaller city with a much different population. With his nearly exclusive white population and our black population, the possibility of an exchange program was appealing to both of us. An unforgettable experience evolved, as each group chose a short article. We traveled to each other's school to read and discuss this article with a new group of friends. When our students first approached this Beloit school, they were apprehensive about going in. This was a different setting, and they didn't know what to expect. Once in the building, however, all fears were forgotten as the host students graciously welcomed the MVS students and gave them a tour of their school. Immediately, they were all just children sharing conversation as if they had known each other for years. Lunch was provided, and the conversation never slowed down.

The first article discussed related to Japanese internment camps. Both groups read and discussed issues concerning how the Japanese were treated in the late 1930s and early 1940s. The book club discussion went extremely well, with all students participating eloquently in the discussion. Time flew by, and the MVS students were ready to board the bus for the return trip home. Good-byes and hugs were shared and plans to meet again at the Village were made.

The return trip had Beloit students going into the inner city of Milwaukee to join their MVS friends to share another article. Concerned about their safety, one Beloit student questioned how close the bus would come to the school entrance. A clearly nervous group of students hesitantly got off their bus and headed directly to the school. Apprehension turned to hugs as soon as the Beloit students saw familiar MVS faces. They immediately became reacquainted and the fellowship, camaraderie, and joy of reading repeated itself in our "house." Again, articles focusing on interpersonal relationships involved all students in positive, in-depth discussions that went on throughout the day. And again, time flew by way too fast. The Beloit students wanted to stay just a little longer, but necessity prevailed, and they were on their way with yet another positive experience to remember.

While brainstorming a culminating activity, Chante, April, and Ngozie insisted that, since Oprah always gave a dinner party to discuss books, why shouldn't we? Moving into action, they, along with students from Beloit, decided to have a dinner party/book discussion at a resort halfway between the schools on a beautiful lake. The consensus among the students of both schools was that they would read Grove's *Crystal Gardens*, an enjoyable book about teenagers learning to get along under unusual circumstances.

Through a grant, all students from both schools were given a copy of the book, while the MVS students shared actual crystal gardens they made as a connected science project with their friends from Beloit. Both groups arrived at this beautiful lakeside resort with no apprehensions or concerns. They just shared their reading and their crystal garden science projects and enjoyed the time with friends. In-depth discussions continued until time ran out. The joy of reading again prevailed as the dominant activity. Everyone thoroughly enjoyed this dinner party.

Do not think for a moment that students Chante, April, and Ngozie were ready to pack up their paper, pencils, and telephones and simply be students again after this great activity. Centering on the needs of the community, their next discussion focused on transferring their joy of reading into neighborhood homes. They decided everyone should have a home library, and they were going to do something about it. The students wrote a grant proposal to remedy the situation. Choosing the Oprah Book of the Month format, each book was to be read by a special guest and copies would be given to students and their families for their home libraries. The grant proposal written and funding received, the girls took action by contacting Carla Allison, proprietor of the neighborhood Readers Choice

Bookstore. Upon explaining the project, Ms. Allison agreed to partner with the school and helped the girls develop a monthly topical schedule of books. Hoping to hook an entire family into reading and discussing books with their children, the girls flew into action. They contacted readers, set up schedules, sent letters, and planned and set up the activities. At the events, they introduced guests and coordinated the free book drawing. Chante Strelke says, "It was student based. . . . We chose what we wanted to read."

Guests came in on a regular basis, providing strong role models for children. A columnist for the *Milwaukee Journal-Sentinel*, Joyce Evans, captured the attention of every student with her reading. She was one of the first invited guest readers. Following her, student April Love's presentation of a poem she had written entitled "When I Am Alone" left staff and students alike speechless:

When I'm alone, I start to read
When I'm alone there's so many things to do sometimes I sit around and polish my shoes.
When I'm alone I play with my Teddy Bear
Sometimes I look out the window and stare
Sometimes I look at the pretty stars so bright
I think what a pretty sight.
When I'm alone I'm not afraid
Because I have God on my side. Before I close my eyes to sleep I get on my knees and pray.

Taken by the beauty of the poem, Ms. Evans featured April in her column "Every Day People" the very next week, stating, "April could be the next Maya Angelou." In a later article, she featured Chante and her mother, Faith (Johnson) Bugg, as an example of how a parent's involvement can lead to strong reading skills. "Her mother is involved in all of the school's programs," wrote Ms. Evans. "She has taught Chante to read a book a day and the importance of school. Ms. (Johnson) Bugg, who will be involved at Chante's school again this year, says she doesn't have to push Chante to do well in school or read. 'I say just because we live in the ghetto we don't have to be of the ghetto.' Chante is a living inspiration for children to read." It's amazing how people have a positive influence on children and may not even know it. As Chante, April, and Ngozie chose the readers, made the calls, and introduced speakers, they developed their leadership skills, as well as their reading skills.

Eugene Kane, also from the *Milwaukee Journal-Sentinel*, came in as a guest to read "Lion King" and give his insight with comparisons to real life. Carla Allison, speaking to Chante and April several years later, said, "Do you remember when Eugene Kane came in to read? Wasn't that wonderful? He really enjoyed it."

Chante said, "We really enjoyed it, listening to people read motivated us to read also."

April added, "There were times in middle school when we were shy to read, but once we got with groups, we learned how to express ourselves, so now . . . being seniors in high school, we can go read and express ourselves on higher levels."

"Now I go down to the library and read just for fun," Chante said. There were more and more guest readers coming into the club, and they seemed to enjoy it as much as the children.

As the culminating event, a four-hour read-in was held. The girls invited all students to read with student book club members who participated on assigned shifts. Drawings were held throughout the read-in, and the students received yet another book for their home libraries. Throughout the year, not one chapter test was held, nor was a textbook ever opened with this group.

> *The earliest and most often forgotten step to learning reading is being read to. Modeling reading can have a strong impact on students.*

Seeking the joy of reading, a goal is to make a wonderful story come alive. "Letting in the Jungle" by Rudyard Kipling was chosen to be the literature read from *Junior Great Books*. This selection truly integrated the arts with academics. Assisted by artist-in-residence Ann Kingsbury and art specialist Roxane Mayeur, all students studied the selection, wrote about the characters, drew or sketched their favorites, and finally created a piece of art that would reflect their memory of the story. A writing booklet, drawn from the literature and complete with sketches, was an excellent addition to their student portfolios, while large-scale artwork was painted on huge windows running the length of the room.

Beginning with a hands-on art experience, the culminating activity included every student in the school. Guided by Ann Kingsbury, a final sketch was prepared by all for eventual transfer to 6" × 6" ceramic tiles. After the tiles were fired, a composite mural was developed and installed on an entry wall of our school during the summer. In fall, at the beginning of the next school year, it was covered with large sheets of paper for a formal unveiling ceremony for students and parents to celebrate their success. To this day, that mural stands, each tile signed by its student artist, as a reminder that these pioneers knew the joy of learning, and it didn't have to be boring.

> *If children are behind in reading, you work on reading. The indicator of success is not that they gain a grade level or two, but that they inherit the joy of reading.*

- Reading
  — Chosen from *Junior Great Books*, "Letting in the Jungle" by Rudyard Kipling
- Materials
  — The story "Letting in the Jungle"
  — Maps of the area where the story takes place
  — Art supplies
    — Sketch pad for all students
    — Ceramic tiles
    — Materials for glazing and firing
- Model: Integrate art and literature
  — Reading and discussion will initially take place in the classroom.
  — Discussion and artistic expression will take place in the art room.
  — The final project will include hands-on art experience and writing samples.
- Beginning the project
  — Introduce the story.
  — Introduce the characters.
  — Read and discuss portions of the story.

- Story mapping
  - Get a large sheet of paper and add characters as they are introduced.
  - Add descriptors as needed so students get an image of each.
  - Talk about the story's setting.
  - Have students write a short narrative about the pages read.
- Completion
  - Tiles are permanently installed.
  - Students will receive a copy of their artwork for their portfolios.
  - Students prepare a writing sample for their portfolios.

LEARNING FROM THE EXPERTS

MVS did not represent the boxed-in world of education. We proceeded to generalize student skills by practicing them out of the classroom and often in business ventures. Teachable moments are found everywhere the minute students step out of the building. To gain a better understanding of the working world, it seemed only logical that students would go into businesses and talk to the experts who do their jobs on a day-to-day basis. As a regular routine and to increase focus, students, in the classroom, prepared to go into a business and talked and wrote about it when they returned to school. Processing, thinking through what they have learned, is integral to the learning process.

- In the classroom before entering a business, students did the following:
  - They reiterated the specific goals and objectives of the experience.
  - They experienced and observed school skills connecting to a real working environment.
- Entering a business, students responded to the following questions:
  - What does this business do?
  - What are the duties of the staff?
  - As a student what can you do for the business?
  - What experiences can the business contribute to our school and students?

The learning goes on and on, and local business becomes an extension of the classroom.

- Returning from the business, students processed their experiences by discussing issues:
  — Today I learned . . .
  — The people who helped me learn were . . .
  — The character skills I practiced today were . . .

Finally, students ranked themselves on how well they felt they responded at the business. Did they ask good questions, understand the roles of the various workers, respond in a business like manner, and so forth? They were usually honest and explained exactly how they wanted to improve.

Potential business partners were everywhere and were of a wide variety. A simple walk around the neighborhood helped locate some small businesses. The local garage's car wash, a day care center, and a corner store were MVS neighbors. A short conversation between the proprietor, students, and teacher would determine how the company would be included in the school's educational plan. After a discussion with the neighboring day care center, Wanita took on the task of organizing a work crew to beautify the grounds as a community service. In exchange, another business, Will's Farm Market, provided expertise to complete the job.

The Village view of business partners was much different from that of most schools. We never asked for money from the business. If money was needed, we would team with the business to develop a grant proposal. We wanted the expertise the business had to offer. Each business did what that business did best and taught our students the skills necessary to do their job. Connections were made in a variety of ways. Having students walk around the neighborhood made the day care connection possible. Every resource was used to procure partners to teach our students.

I (MGB) had previously brought students to MATA Media Communications to develop television programs. MATA is Milwaukee's community access programming. Students operated equipment, as well as performed in front of the camera in one way or another. Executive director Vel Wiley had written a letter of support for the proposal of our school. "As an organization that encourages community growth and education, I also offer any assistance that MATA can provide in the education and development of telecommunication and computer skills for the children, educators and parents." Ms. Wiley met with us to discuss how we could collaborate to accomplish a wide range of student goals. She had a long-time interest in city kids and a reputation as an involved community leader. She wanted youths to be part of the programming at the MATA television studios, and MVS was ready and willing to participate.

Incorporated into our first yearly plan, every student in our school was to experience eight days in the television production studio for training, preparation, learning camera skills, and the taping of a final product. Chante remembers:

> We had to figure out a public service announcement. First we were in the classroom and we had to choose a topic: violence prevention or anything we wanted. We broke up into groups and we worked on the topic. We worked on the script, and everything needed to create this public service announcement. It was like a little movie, I call it. We then went down to MATA, and they showed us how to use everything, like how to use the cameras, how to edit, how to work the soundboard. Everything about a television production.

The group decided to develop a program concept related to alcohol and drug abuse that eventually evolved into the writing of their public-service announcement. Writing, rewriting, and detailed preparation were the orders of the day, as the final product had to be worthy of a real television presentation. Leaving for their eight-day experience at MATA, scripts in hand, they put on their business faces and were ready to go. Guiding students through their daily assignments, the MATA staff members were adept trainers. Taping was done on the final day, and students had various jobs in the studio. It was a thrill to see students blossom in their skills and abilities, working as the cameraperson, floor manager, sound technician, and director. Everyone had a part, and each student preferred a different aspect of the project. The boisterous student who longed for a stage was the main actor, confidently delivering her scripted dialogue in front of a camera. The shy student was focusing the $5,000 camera and taking directions from the student floor manager. The aspiring rap artist worked on a sound mixing board with avid attention to the floor manager. This project prompted MATA director Vel Wiley to say to students, "That public service announcement you did was an exciting experience. Now that was an English assignment wasn't it?"

To write, rewrite, and rewrite is better than a writing class. There is something for everyone in projects like this, and students are reading, writing, speaking, and doing math and science more than ever.

The generalization of skills is why it is important for children to get into the community. The natural joy of learning that comes with it will give them a leg up in life and in college.

CELEBRATIONS OF LEARNING

Celebrations and demonstrations of learning are the backbone of a strong educational philosophy. Thomas Armstrong, in *Multiple Intelligences in the Classroom*, lists twenty-three various ways "to show that I know," and celebrates each and every one of them. "Exhibitions," one term for the celebration and demonstration of learning, can be used as the culminating activity for an educational theme. What a great way to integrate the arts with academic learning. This exhibition can take many forms. A science fair is the most common, with students standing by their exhibits to hawk their skills. A unique way to demonstrate learning is with a short play, puppet show, or musical presentation. Individual speeches and presentations are extremely valuable and make a great promotion assessment. There are many creative ways to demonstrate and celebrate what is learned. Some are in front of the whole school in an auditorium and some are simply in the classroom in front of classmates. Let the imagination run wild, and students will demonstrate what they really know.

At MVS, exhibitions followed each of the six themes we had during the year. One was especially memorable. As students were ushered into the room, it was evident that they would be trying something new. A backdrop, five feet tall, was full of student artwork relating to the sights of various locations on the continent of Africa. Standing in front of the backdrop was Robert, fully dressed in a tuxedo, ready to be the master of ceremonies. Robert opened the activities by welcoming the audience and introducing Ms. Black's class, the animal experts. From behind the backdrop, up popped a cardboard puppet of a gorilla held on a stick, while Robert supplied its voice.

"Hi, I live up to thirty-three years and grow to eight feet tall. The females only grow to six feet. I am a lowland gorilla."

Following this act, on the upper corner of the backdrop, stage right, was a cutout of a crocodile. The mouth opened and shut by a mechanism held backstage. Andre operated the mouth and was also the voice of the crocodile.

"I'm a crocodile. I live in the rain forest, and I have babies. They always bother me."

Andre's ambition was to become a stand-up comic. Appreciating the laughter, Andre continued.

"I put the babies in my mouth to help them hatch. When full grown, I will be twenty-five feet long. When small animals come within my reach, I eat them. They taste great. I love my life. I have to go back in the water now. Bye."

Exhibitions are wide-ranging and flexible. They can be presented any time and any place, but most often serve as the culminating activity of a theme. They can include everything from a Greek fashion show to a mathematical demonstration. Presentations by students to students, such as a demonstration of geometric home designs, an African play in a marketplace, or programs that showcase students' music or dance skills, can be used in conjunction with participatory events like science, health, or job fairs. Do students remember these? Ask them in two or three years, and they will tell you. They will remember something that involved social interaction or something they really did, such as build a model, design a mural, develop a musical, put on a demonstration, prepare a photo essay, or teach something to someone else.

An abandonment of adult-led school assemblies, exhibitions are presented by and for students. Now don't believe for one second this is easy. These activities were practiced and repracticed. Teacher Harry Collins states, "Exhibitions are great because they keep the teachers focused on the subject matter. They have to teach, or their class looks stupid." Be certain that children know and can demonstrate subject matter. This gives a stronger focus to both the teacher and the student and requires true accountability. How embarrassing if students are sent in front of the whole student body unprepared!

At MVS, our first exhibitions were pretty shabby, but improvement came with every attempt, and students showed increased pride in their work. Seeing what could be accomplished, students insisted on being totally prepared. These demonstrations of learning help put the focus where it belongs, with students fully involved in every aspect of their education. These creative ideas only come when we choose to look at the world in different ways.

> The exhibition keeps children and teachers focused on results. It is very difficult for anyone to fake it when a teacher's students are standing in front of an audience.

CHAPTER 4

Designing an Educational System for Children: What a Novel Thought

In order to make changes in the way we educate children, we must make dramatic changes in the way the educational process is designed. How do we implement an educational philosophy and system that opens the doorway to learning so essential in today's world? How do we allow children and teachers to take control of their educational lives? We completely erase from our minds the way schools are "spozed" to be and start over, focusing on how to build an effective educational design that holds on to all children. To achieve this, change must be dramatic. We can no longer tinker with reform. Recognizing that most rules are not really rules anyway, we surge forward with clear minds and with children in our hearts, and we start to break the mold.

The first important step in redesigning education is to take a sledgehammer to the rigid curriculum and time frames of the past. With parents and students leading the way, the goal is to design a localized curriculum in the form of a list of fundamental, usable skills that will be helpful to children as they grow. No longer must every sixth grader be on page fifty-two of the sixth-grade textbook by October 10. No longer will students simply memorize irrelevant facts for a chapter test. Once we scrap the textbook as the curriculum, learning can now come from everywhere, and the demonstration of learning will replace memorization in this redesigned educational structure.

Where should the curriculum come from? From local educators, community members, parents, and students of course. It is essential to the redesign of a school that a curriculum be planned locally, with regard to the needs of the children being served. It is essential that students become proficient in RWA, or reading, writing, and arithmetic, but a clear path to attaining these skills is not contained in an edict sent down from a central administration, a state department, or the federal government. It is not controlled by a bubble-sheet test; nor do textbook companies control it. This curriculum is developed locally and individually adapted to continually meet the specific needs of children, using state and national norms as guidelines.

CHARTING THE COURSE

Paper hung all over the walls and ideas poured out from every direction as we produced the beginnings of a curriculum that manifested itself in the form of a proficiency list. As the design for the school's curriculum, this list emphasized the fundamental educational needs of children. It was a little ragtag at first, but changes occurred throughout the years. We started by listing everything students needed to know, what they needed to do, and how students needed to be, and then proceeded to put the items listed into categories consistent with the public school system. We were still under their control. This representation is a reverse of the past method, when headings included math, English, and social studies, for instance, and individual goals were placed under those headings. We erased from our minds what a curriculum was "spozed" to be and started from the bottom up. After combining and sorting many times over, we ended up with six categories and nine pages of goals under them. Although our list was creative, the confines of a large public school system were evident and forced us into a somewhat traditional mode. Remember, we did not have one final requirement; we had many, and they were usable skills. Here are just a few random samples:

1. Communication skills
    a. Reading
        i.   Gain information from newspapers and magazines.

       ii. Interpret forms, personal information, and financial agreements.

       iii. Use a road and street map.

       iv. Interpret information from research material resources.

   b. Writing

       i. Identify incorrect punctuation.

       ii. Write a resume and a personal-information sheet.

       iii. Write an autobiography.

       iv. Write a research paper on a topic of your choosing, develop techniques for selecting subjects, and identify purposes and audience.

   c. Speaking

       i. Speak with acceptable pronunciation.

       ii. Use language that is clear and direct.

       iii. Learn the fundamentals of group discussion.

       iv. Give an effective oral opinion presentation on a subject of your choosing.

   d. Listening

       i. Demonstrate attentive and active listening.

       ii. Determine main ideas from a discussion.

       iii. Pick out supporting evidence in a presentation.

       iv. Follow a thought and summarize information.

   e. Arts (one of the following)

       i. Demonstrate the ability to read music.

       ii. Memorize and read a script.

       iii. Demonstrate communication through a dance routine.

       iv. Create visual-symbolic representations to convey information.

2. Problem solving and analytical thinking

   a. Computing

       i. Compare fractions, decimals, and percentages in a usable way.

       ii. Use metric measurement in calculations and conversions.

       iii. Use logic or an algebraic equation to solve a real problem of your choosing.

   b. Information access and processing
      i.   Demonstrate the ability to use a computer to gather information.
      ii. Gather information to solve a problem of your choosing.
      iii. Demonstrate the ability to use a variety of reference tools (e.g., periodical index, encyclopedia, Internet)
   c. Science processes
      i.   Gather and record scientific data using rulers, balances, and timing devices.
      ii. Use a graduated cylinder to measure the volume of a liquid.
      iii. Apply the scientific method in a project that is real to you.
      iv. Gather and interpret data, draw scientific conclusions, and make predictions based on the data about a subject that is real to you.
3. Technical skills
   a. Computer technology
      i.   Demonstrate the ability to use the word processor effectively.
      ii. Use science data to make charts and bar graphs on the computer to help explain a point.
      iii. Compute data on Excel or a similar program.
      iv. Demonstrate the ability to gather information on the Internet.
   b. Use of hand tools
      i.   Show effective use of simple household tools.
      ii. Demonstrate safe and effective handling of simple power tools used in everyday life.
      iii. Use proper measurement.
   c. Audiovisual devices
      i.   Show an ability to use a handheld video camera.
      ii. Demonstrate skills in transferring videotape.
      iii. Use a store-style scanner to enhance a photograph.
4. Physical and emotional wellness
   a. Health

      i.   Prepare a meal that is part of a balanced diet.

      ii. Demonstrate proper dental care.

      iii. Be aware of the effect of alcohol, drugs, and tobacco on the body.

      iv. Practice proper hygiene.

  b. Physical fitness

      i.   Demonstrate body strength and proper technique in lifting heavy items.

      ii. Learn how to play a variety of lifelong physical games (e.g., basketball, badminton).

      iii. Learn techniques to maintain cardiovascular fitness during the aging process.

      iv. Learn basic skills in dance.

  c. Interpersonal skills

      i.   Role-play healthy ways of dealing with anger.

      ii. Describe how people are unique in the way they look and act.

      iii. Demonstrate general attitudes and behaviors that help people relate to others.

      iv. Identify characteristics of confident behavior.

5. Community awareness

  a. Community resources

      i.   Map and know your neighborhood.

      ii. Determine the best form of public transportation needed to travel in or out of your city.

      iii. Show how to access community health services.

      iv. Compare schedules and costs to determine the best form of out-of-town travel.

  b. Government

      i.   Demonstrate how and where to apply for a variety of permits.

      ii. Demonstrate how to register and to vote.

      iii. Describe the checks and balances and separation of powers of government.

      iv. Access your government representatives.

  c. Consumer economic

      i.   Identify major points in renting or buying a home.

      ii. Demonstrate the ability to estimate costs when shopping.

     iii. Demonstrate a basic understanding of available banking services.

     iv. Develop a household budget.

6. Professional preparation

  a. Work and career planning

      i. Explore jobs to assist you in making your choice.

      ii. Understand the concept of the business cycle.

     iii. Understand where and how to get local labor-market information.

     iv. Develop career goals, understanding that they may change.

  b. Employment skills

      i. Complete a resume and job application.

      ii. Show success in mock job interviews.

     iii. Know how to dress for success.

     iv. Demonstrate knowledge of resources needed to procure potential jobs, such as community job-placement bureaus and the like.

  c. Character development skills

      i. Demonstrate through role playing, home practice, and everyday living the following skills:

- Asking for help
- Expressing your feelings
- Using self-control
- Dealing with an accusation

The following is an example of the checklist format, which documents what was taught and when, as well as when it was demonstrated by the student.

Attempt	Attempt	Completion	Assignment
9/23/96	_____	_____	Demonstrate independent use of the scientific method through the construction of projects, experiments, and exploration

Comments: Student needs to focus on making a clear definition of the problem before proceeding.

Community awareness
Community resources

Attempt	Attempt	Completion	Assignment
10/17/96	_____	10/24/96	Map your neighborhood

Comments: Student meets proficiency. Can properly map neighborhood using all correct street names and locations.

As students move through the list, place dates on the checklist lines to acknowledge student attempts and completion with continuous comments indicating where the students need to focus. Students never fail if they don't complete their goals; they simply never stop trying until they reach it. Ideally, this list is reviewed and altered every year. All stakeholders are included and the emphasis is placed where it belongs, on the child and parent. When we first released this form at MVS, we heard a variety of comments from parents, from "What is this doing on the checklist, I don't want my child learning this," to "This is great, I finally know what my child is learning." The more you make parents part of the real process, the more they will know how to support their children and school. These proficiencies can be demonstrated in any way throughout the student's school years. It is also clear that movement away from these goals is acceptable as individual plans may be made with parents, and the program adapted to the student's needs. Not every student has to do the same thing in the same way at the same time. Review the individualized checklist for each student as he or she approaches completion. This will ensure that the student is meeting the goals necessary for his or her future. When designing a student's checklist, remember, less is more; it is concepts that are important. What are traditionally called the middle school portion and the high school portion of the secondary school program are blended together in this unique philosophy to keep the flow of education moving without rigid time frames designed to fail students and hold them in an "area" such as middle school. If a student has completed his or her individual goals designed around guidelines, that student is ready to leave secondary school, whenever that may be. If students need more time, they can stay longer, that is, through grade thirteen. The thirteen-year school is common in Canada and other foreign countries.

Standards become guidelines for success, rather than deadlines for failure.

Suggestions for students' leaving high school are:

1. The student will complete his or her individualized checklist.
2. The student will complete a portfolio demonstrating accomplishments.
3. The student will make a final presentation of choice. This presentation can take any form the student chooses and is made, with the student fully prepared, in front of an audience.

Completion of each of these activities will demonstrate competency in strong individual skill areas like communication skills, problem solving, and analytical thinking, as well as in the remainder of the proficiency areas. Growth charts, line graphs of progress toward an individual goal, clearly show forward gains in knowledge. It is essential that we not go back to an era where students are promoted without gains, especially in reading. The results we show are students who can actually demonstrate progress in what they know and parents who are right beside them during the process.

Have a wide range of parents, educators, community members, and students review the curriculum checklist yearly and recommend adjustments. Then, have the program individualized, with the fundamentals remaining solid. The goal remains to take all children to their highest levels. Never again can we allow children to move through a system without learning.

A criticism of integrated, project-based, and community-based learning is that not enough quality time is spent on the fundamentals of English, math, science, social studies, and the like. Many believe students need specialized teachers and separate classes in order to learn. These concerns can be answered by planning a creative curriculum with the prevailing thought that experiential learning is much broader than the narrow scope of the textbook. However, a strong focus must be maintained on the basic academic objectives so they do not get lost in the process. To ensure the inclusion of all fundamental academics, the planning of projects must be a team effort. In a two-teacher team, English is often paired with social studies and math with science. Teachers on the team have expertise in two major subjects or must seek support in these areas. As activities are planned, each teacher reverts to the proficiency benchmark list to ensure all objectives of the subject areas are covered. This replaces separate classes and keeps the focus on the learning of fundamental academics.

Don't think for one minute that this philosophy excludes higher-level learning. It is clearly built into the benchmark checklist. For those who are advanced in one area or another, be certain that this philosophy goes beyond minimal academic requirements. In addition to staff expertise, utilize community experts, including professionals, tradespeople, and university staff as a support. Let higher-level skills come from those who know them best, those who use them daily. When higher-level skills become job specific, have experts address them. Not only do students achieve high-level skills, they explore the skills based on their interests without the evil shadow of failure haunting them at every turn. How many students with the potential of Albert Einstein or Isaac Newton are there, who simply need the chance to demonstrate their abilities in a nonthreatening environment? In *Growing Up in New Guinea*, Margaret Mead wrote, "My grandmother wanted me to have an education so she kept me out of school." Maybe it's time to allow learning to happen in school and wherever school takes us.

The proficiency list gives direction to the curriculum and, there-
fore, to daily projects. Although there is much more to learn in
order to prepare for life than subject matter, academic objectives
of fundamental importance must not get lost. Increased higher-
level learning skills must be made available to students in unique
ways.

AND WHAT GRADE ARE YOU REALLY IN?

Upon review of a wide range of assessments, it becomes evident that all students simply do not fit into the same mold. While some develop more rapidly in math, they may progress at a slower rate in reading. Others might develop faster in reading and more slowly in math. What is clear, however, is that nobody is on the same page of the textbook at the same time. This is nothing new. It has been the case for years, and educators have just refused to deal with it. If we focus on academic standards, to what grade would we assign students? When we enroll sixth-grade children reading at the third-grade level, do we continue to give them a sixth-grade text to read, or do we open up a third grade for placement there? But wait a minute, what if the child's math skills are more like those of a ninth grader and the child has the musical skills of a concert pianist? In which grade should the child be placed? What does third-grade level of reading mean anyway?

The reality is, when attention is paid to each child, grade levels
become obsolete. Students are kept in classes with their peers and
taught based on their individual needs.

These differences in learning rates and ways must be built into the curriculum's design. It is a great error to believe that by simply carrying a sixth-grade text, a child will automatically read on the sixth-grade level. We are teaching children, and the charge is to bring them along, one step at a time, from where they are. We must make a commitment to develop a flow of learning that does not allow educators ever to give up on a child. Susan Ohanian, in her article for *Kappan Magazine* in December 1996, likens students' learning to the dripping of sap from a maple tree: "Even in these days of instant everything, you can't hurry maple syrup—or third graders or seventh graders. Children learn one drop at a time." They learn at their speed, when they decide to. This does not mean that students are allowed to muddle through, progressing at their slowest rate. It simply means they progress at their fastest rate, encouraged at every possible moment and pressured when necessary, to ensure their best progress. Time lines are used as guidelines for achievement, rather than deadlines for failure.

We only have to take a close look at today's educational design to discover a major underlying flaw in the learning process. Following the mathematics curriculum for example, every student must be on the same page at the same time, especially when the chapter test is given. The curriculum has a time line designed to fail students if they are not learning as fast as others. Even worse, students who miss one concept on a test may never get another chance to learn it. Think about it. When the test is over, the whole class moves on to the next chapter.

As a volunteer in a fifth-grade classroom, I (EL) worked with Arthur on his math two days a week. He had just finished a test and survived it with a C. I guess that means he is average. I was given the choice of two ways to help him. I could work on the information needed for his next test, helping him to get a better grade, or I could help him with the problems he had not understood on the test just completed. This was an easy choice for me. If I didn't help him with the problems he had missed on the earlier test, who would? Absolutely no one! And then what would happen next year in middle school? He would start out behind with less and less chance of catching up.

Imagine the massive reality of this thought; every student who misses one concept or more on a chapter math test, does not get a chance, that year, to learn it. In a system of one hundred thousand students, it's safe to say that 80 percent miss one concept on each of the chapter tests. That makes about eighty thousand children left behind. If there are twenty chapter tests, that leaves 1.6 million concepts being missed each year. What about reading? We do the same things. At the end of second grade, ready or not, the students move on to third grade, and they are expected to read on that level. Those who haven't progressed as rapidly as others start out behind, and they stay behind as the standard goes higher and higher. How do we make individual time lines for everyone and take children from where they are?

We do it by designing a framework that allows teachers to focus on individual differences, and we start by eliminating the concept of grade levels.

DEVELOPING A FLOW OF LEARNING

At MVS, we assigned middle school–aged students to teams and created the atmosphere of the one-room schoolhouse, with student ages ranging from approximately eleven to thirteen. Didn't this create a problem with children of different ages in the same classroom? Let's take a look at the ages of children in those grade levels today. Due to student failure, illness, and various starting times, there already exists a wide range of ages in each grade level. With the addition of a high school element, however, fourteen- through eighteen-year-olds would be separate from the middle school. Under the current system, grade levels define student progress. If students barely pass enough seventh-grade courses, they become eighth graders, regardless of what they have or have not learned. If they don't pass, they remain behind as older students in a younger class. How about allowing demonstrated learning to define student progress. If a student could do advanced work in mathematics, she or he would get work in advanced mathematics. If slow readers progress from where they are rather than being forced into an eighth-grade text they aren't yet ready to read, they then can improve in reading without being left behind. If we did those things, we would then be able to focus on the progress of children using authentic assessment to chart their educational flow. Readers would never again be left behind simply because they hadn't jumped up grade levels under the false assumption that they had completed the necessary skills. In addition, students would not be devastated by a system of failure that eventually leads to more dropouts.

Of those entering the sixth grade at MVS, 80 percent were dramatically behind in reading. Many of them were on the second-grade reading level according to our assessment. In most schools, they would have been expected to function with a sixth-grade text, whether or not they could read it. At MVS, we accepted the reality of their levels and, for reading, grouped them together. We wanted to make reading enjoyable for them, but we also wanted them to be comfortable in their groups. We didn't make a big fuss about their levels; we didn't call them stupid; we didn't even discuss the issue. We just celebrated their gains, and in the 1997–1998 school year, 75 percent made dramatic gains. Compare this with the 20 percent who had ever made that accomplishment prior to coming to our school. It worked. None of the children complained about their group, and they enjoyed every minute.

To maintain a constant flow of learning, it is essential that no one fail the whole grade. What would be the purpose other than an educational tradition of telling children they are stupid and putting them farther and farther behind? Under our philosophy, no matter what grade students are supposed to be in, we teach them from where they are. At MVS, we simply had no grade levels. The current system didn't allow such a thing to happen, but again, we simply broke the rules. At MVS, we ignored grade levels; when it came time to do the administrative paperwork, no one failed a whole grade. Farmer Will Allen, talking to MVS students about their Greenhouse Project, said:

> I know you guys have grown some stuff that wasn't as successful, and that's part of the process. It's kind of a nurturing thing too, learning that not everything is going to be successful in life, learning how to recover from failure. Because as a farmer, I farm over one hundred acres, not everything works out. That's the way life is. I have to recover from failure of this crop, plant another crop, go back and figure out what happened with the soil. It's a lot of discovery stuff that we learn.

> *Failure is a natural part of learning. It can no longer be made a horrible, devastating thing.*

Positive failure must be everyday business, done on a day-to-day basis.

Going back to Arthur, my math student. When I asked him questions about his work, he would continuously hesitate.

"Why are you hesitating, Arthur? You know this answer," I said.

"I don't want to miss it. I don't want to get the wrong answer," he replied.

"You already know this answer," I said. "What is it?"

Arthur started to answer, "Well, the answer is four, oh I mean . . ."

He stopped short and looked at me for approval. I did not respond, and he continued. "No, I mean six." He looked up again, but I remained silent. "No, I mean . . ."

I interrupted. By this time, he had no idea what the problem was, not to mention the answer.

"Slow down, Arthur. Start over, look at the numbers and relax," I said. "Ok, thirty-six divided by nine. Now, nine can't go into three, so how many times can it go into thirty-six?"

"One nine is nine. Two nine's are . . . The answer is four," he said hesitantly.

"Is that your final answer, Arthur?" I asked, "Are you sure?"

"Well, I think it is," and he started to figure it again.

"Right answer," I said, "and you had it the very first time."

From that point on, we worked on skills and confidence. When asked why he didn't stay with his first answer, he said, "I'm afraid to be wrong." There's nothing bad about being wrong. Failure is a part of learning. A special note for the straight-A students, those who don't fail and don't get anything wrong on their tests: They are capable of learning a whole lot more; they are simply not being challenged.

> *By eliminating grade levels as an indicator of academic progress, and by keeping a strong focus on real assessment, not only will we never again leave children behind, we will never again keep an advanced child from moving forward.*

Additional benefits come from eliminating grade levels. Students can now remain in the same class for three years, allowing a bond to form between teachers and the students' families. Bonding develops trust, and the trust between parents, students, and teachers can only be enhanced over a period of time. This is especially significant during the difficult middle school years. Grade levels have too long been used as a vehicle to dump children into the unending cycle of failure. Students who get older, and especially males who grow physically larger, are moved on to read a seventh-grade text with second-grade skills. No longer can this dumping continue. It is essential that we hold onto every child and maintain the flow of learning to ensure that all children show progress from where they are.

When you develop a flow of learning that includes everyone, grade levels become obsolete, allowing a continuous flow of learning to exist.

CHANGING TIME FRAMES

Quality time is essential to learning and must be available when teachable moments occur. Teachable moments rarely happen on schedule and definitely not on a limited schedule. In our educational design, the teachers on the team plan the schedule daily, based on what needs to be accomplished. This means no more blocked-out forty-five minute classes. Designing a flexible daily schedule allows educators the freedom to focus on the learning needs of students. If time is needed for students to complete a project effectively, they complete the project rather than move to a math or English class. If time is needed to take the classroom into the community, a forty-five minute class will not restrict it. The only way to comply with the current standards of the education of minutes is to abandon projects, integrated learning, and community experiences and to call each forty minutes a class dedicated solely to an isolated subject area. Minute learning forces a teaching style on quality educators who must then discard elements of creativity essential to the process of learning. Once educators stop caring how many minutes are devoted to each subject, the focus of a good teacher automatically goes toward learning. Time will now be geared to the lesson, rather than the lesson geared to the time.

"There is absolutely no believable research to support the notion that an exact amount of 'sitting time' equals an exact amount of learning," states Dr. Ed Pino, who knows the value of quality time in learning.

TEAMING TO LEARN

Our educational design places teachers in two-class teams, allowing flexibility:

- It begins with two-class teams.
- It utilizes those two teachers working with a special education teacher and an educational assistant (or two educational assistants).
  — All adults are simply called teachers because that is what they do.
  — Special education teachers and students are not openly identified.
  — Educational assistants (aides) will follow through on plans made by the teachers.
- It structures average class size as follows:
  — A class size of thirty grows to sixty when the two classes are put together as a team; however, they will have four teachers.
  — Creative utilization of the four adults in this group leads, on average, to a fifteen-to-one adult-student ratio.
  — Teachers, who usually teach five classes per day, see around 150 children. Teachers under this plan see sixty children. This allows more individual attention and better use of teacher time.
- It abandons the traditional mass education of children and develops the concept of working in small groups, thus allowing the most benefit to students.
  — Small groups are utilized for reading.
  — Small groups work on projects.
  — Small groups use the available technology.
  — Small groups are pulled out to address behavioral needs.
  — Small groups go into the community.
- Higher-level learning is achieved where it means the most.
  — It is learned through partnerships with community experts.

In the past, classes were designed in neat eight-period days. When the bell rang, everything stopped, and everyone moved. It was easy, because all students were expected to learn at the same rate in the same way. Teaming is certainly not new. The critical issue, however, is that teachers take charge of their educational lives to create schedules as needed. When a teacher wants to keep her students for a week to do a project emphasizing science skills, all she has to do is plan it with her team. When another wants to separate boys and girls for a specific gender-related activity, no problem; he or she just plans it with the team. When a teacher wants to leave the building with fifteen students, he or she just plans it with the team. Whether you want longer time periods, shorter time periods, smaller groups or larger groups, no problem; just plan it with the team. Time frames no longer control learning.

READING CLUBS

Although projects and community experiences were integrated, reading clubs were an exception. Reading is especially conducive to small groups. As most classes, under this philosophy, contain students with a wide range of reading skills, it is imperative that their specific needs be met. Within the team of students, those with the lowest reading skills would be in the smallest groups and those with the highest reading skills, in the larger groups. At MVS, the teams included two classroom teachers, a special education teacher, and an educational assistant. On an average day, for example, the educational assistant could take four to six low-level readers and follow a teacher's plan to emphasize phonics. The special education teacher could take students with specific reading needs, be they regular or special education needs. This class size could easily be twelve to fourteen students. The two class teachers could then divide the remainder and have a relatively small class of about twenty, including some students with higher-level reading skills. With this flexibility, the team of teachers could come closer to meeting the needs of all the readers, and the teams could change daily, both in size as well as student composition. At MVS, each team had access to small rooms within the Village Square that held ten to twelve students to make learning more accessible.

WORKING ON PROJECTS

Additional creativity may be required to apportion available space within the building to allow students to have enough room to complete a well-planned project. Projects quite often utilize larger groups and are more flexible. Most require a wide range of jobs, making it easier to utilize a range of student skill levels. Depending on the project, groups could be divided in many ways. At MVS, projects often encompassed a large number of students scattered throughout the rooms and spilling into the hall. With a large group of students in many locations, the four teachers could easily disperse throughout the area and attend to all sixty students. Teacher Monique Brown had her thirty students designing and putting together model houses. Two teachers easily supervised her students, scattered throughout her classroom and the halls. They were able to give instruction at the proper level, as well as maintain an educational environment conducive to learning.

USING TECHNOLOGY

What classroom adjustments do we make to serve children under this plan? There are many creative ways to arrange classes under this design. MVS allocated seven computers to each classroom. The utilization of this technology was based on the student's need, rather than the student's schedule. Computer labs serve a purpose, but many of them are located away from daily classroom activities, putting students on the room's schedule, not their own. There will be students whose needs keep them on the computer for longer periods of time, while some need minimal time. Placing seven computers in each classroom allowed for a continuous flow of activities; students moved to the computers and away to other activities based on their needs. At our school, computers become one station within the classroom.

Utilizing the creative classroom plan, essential to the Village philosophy, teacher Doris Black worked on fundamental projects in her classroom. Emphasizing math, those projects took many forms. Dividing her class into four groups, she had each group working at its individual level. A group of seven students worked on the computer using math-related software, while others were involved in projects or other relevant activities at three other stations. Groups rotated stations to complete their assigned activities. The computers were constantly in use, with students remaining at their stations as long as necessary, based on their needs. The same plan was utilized for other technology, such as educational programming on cable television. The flexibility of groups allowed Doris to spend more time with a smaller group doing projects because seven were self-directed at the computers.

BEHAVIORAL NEEDS

It is a fact of life that middle school–aged students don't always act in a manner conducive to the learning environment of the school. The traditional concept of sending a disrupter to an administrator not only creates an added expense in the need to hire more and more administrators, but wastes that student's learning time. In most current school systems, a teacher can use just about every behavioral technique a principal can, except suspension. Often, students are sent to a holding room, where they do absolutely nothing, waiting for an administrator to call home or give one of those famous lectures, the concept being that at least they are out of the classroom and not disrupting others.

Our new concept is that the four teachers have responsibility for the child for several reasons. First, the teacher knows the child and family better than an administrator. Remember, under this philosophy, students stay with a teacher team for three years. Second, the teacher knows the student violation better because she or he saw it happen. And third, and most importantly, every time a teacher sends a child to someone else for discipline, the student perceives that teacher as unable to manage him or her. This dramatically decreases that teacher's ability to be effective.

To support this, administrators must allow the team of teachers flexibility to handle most situations on their own. First, an outside phone line or cellular phone is made available to every team. Phone calls to home are immediate in cases of the need for discipline, as well as for notifying parents of a great accomplishment by their child. Second, the group of four teachers can divide students any way they want to free a teacher to make the appropriate phone call or needed lecture. On a particularly bad behavior day, one teacher might take five or six students away from the class to process what they did and compare it with what they should have done. Not only is the class free from the continuous disruption, but disruptive students work on their own character development. Flexibility is again the key, and the educational responsibility for the student remains where it belongs, with the teachers.

FINDING OUR WAY OUT THE DOOR

A stolen quote from the television show *The Wonder Years* states, "It is the role of the public school teacher to take an otherwise enjoyable activity and zap it of every ounce of pleasure."

My goodness, I (EL) used to fall asleep while doing teacher observations in a high school. If it's that boring for me, how can the children possibly cope? I would like to see every teacher sit through an eight-period day and listen to talking heads tell them what they are "spozed" to learn. Dispelling the myth that education isn't worth anything unless children are miserable, teachers can now set out beyond the four walls to explore the community and locate real learning experiences where they are. What marvelous experiences are in store, and what a great way to allow teachers to teach.

Traditionally, to get a group out of school for a community experience is an administrative nightmare. Teachers must be sought to cover classes, students are pulled out of an array of classes, and the whole learning process is disrupted. Under the flexible plan described here, the team of teachers controls the schedule for the day, and the students stay with that team. Basic to our philosophy, community experiences become a hassle-free activity. No longer do teachers have to stop other activities midstream when the bell rings. Critical to the success of the school, these teachers are the ones who are in the trenches educating children. It's time to take away the roadblocks.

> *No longer can we be held hostage by the boxed-in world of education. No longer can we justify an educational design that stymies teacher and student creativity. An educational design must be developed that allows teachers the freedom to teach and students the freedom to learn.*

KEEPING THE FOCUS: USING THE ENTIRE YEAR TO LEARN

The need to improve student focus, essential to educational development, leads to the decision to plan for a year-round schedule. When students have three months off in the summer, they have regressed, both educationally and behaviorally, when they return to school in the autumn. The original intent of the nine-month school year was to allow children to help on their parent's farm. This is not essential in an urban community in this day and age. In addition, education is disrupted by days off scattered throughout the school year. Often dictated by the birth of a president or a religious holiday, these holidays rarely satisfy teacher or student needs and certainly don't make educational sense. Rarely can work continue with children for six straight weeks without the interruption of one holiday or another or a teacher-planning day. How do we develop a school designed to maintain student focus? We design a year-round school.

We set out to develop an intensive, year-round program for MVS students without increasing the budget. This schedule was designed to include a solid six weeks of school followed by two weeks away from the school setting. Although the two weeks were time off from school, Shawn Hatlelli, the YMCA representative on the Village School Council, suggested a plan designed to continue student education throughout the year. Under this plan, the YMCA would provide a wide range of recreational and educational services during the two-week break, as well as during the three-week summer period. This would be a great collaboration, allowing students to receive education year-round, while providing them with a whole range of services. The six-week sessions at MVS would be concentrated, with no weekdays off, while traditional holidays were built into each two-week break from school. The Milwaukee Village School and Community Center would become a reality with the YMCA running its program both in our school and in its nearby facility. In addition, representatives from the Milwaukee Public Schools Recreation Department also operated within the building and were willing to support us where they could. Additional businesses such as the neighborhood Readers Choice Bookstore would be welcome to run their business out of our school under the community-education concept, while the Isaac Coggs medical clinic already operated within the building. Under this plan, as written into our original proposal, the Milwaukee Village School and Community Center would become a reality.

We presented this concept to all stakeholders, and the Village Council authorized me (EL) to develop a draft schedule and to gather information. We held two parent meetings with input from staff at

Congress Street School, who had experience operating on a year-round schedule. A survey and phone poll of parents indicated 95 percent approved of the program. Students and teachers were also surveyed and agreed to the plan; and yes, the union was fully on board. We made our formal request for full implementation of the new schedule and were excited by the prospect of utilizing the wide range of community resources available in the summer.

A major strength of this proposal was its relative freedom from additional expense, requiring little or no change to MVS budget. The building had a year-round custodial staff already operative. Recreation programs were in existence throughout the year, and Ulla Pinion, our phenomenal school secretary, was already a twelve-month employee. Accommodations would have to be made for some employees, such as teachers and food-service personnel, but this was all workable. It had been difficult to justify those empty classrooms all summer long. Factoring in the cost of wasted empty classrooms makes the plan financially workable, and if the older students needed to work a job, we would make it a part of the curriculum.

As we approached a meeting with a wide range of central administration department heads, we wondered who would get in the way. There were way too many central office types to allow a complete consensus. It was amazing, however, that only one department put a halt to this portion of our dream. Everyone else was supportive. Now get your paper and pencils ready because I'm going to give you a quiz. Of all the central office departments, only one got in the way. Was it Food Service? Building and Maintenance? Administrative Services? Payroll? Or Labor Relations? Tick tock tick tock tick tock, time's up. Put your pencils down. The answer is (drum roll, please) Payroll. They couldn't or wouldn't find a way to pay teachers on a twelve-month basis. They had been able to work it out for the Congress School program, but it seemed no other exceptions would be made. This portion of the dream was left unfulfilled for a while, but good guy Deputy Superintendent Tom McGinnity, along with the Payroll staff, started the ball rolling to develop a new payroll system, allowing flexible teacher pay schedules.

This plan was eventually implemented a few years later, when our good friend, principal Martha Wheeler-Fair, made her school, Francis Starms Learning Center, the first official year-round school under the new payroll plan. We had left the school by then, but at least we paved the way for others.

You might not win every battle immediately, but if the seeds are planted, you will pave the way for the future.

TRASHING THE BRANDING IRON

As visitors entered MVS, they had to look long and hard to find the special education wing of the building. Should they have looked in the basement? Maybe they should have looked in a converted mobile classroom outside. Where were those "special" children? If the truth be known, they were everywhere, but they were difficult for an occasional observer to identify.

Yes, a visitor may have observed students demonstrating their special needs through their behaviors, their appearance, or the speed at which they learned, but MVS did not brand them for easy identification by all. The philosophical difference is that we didn't believe in the concept of "inclusion." This concept was originally designed to allow children with special education needs to be educated in their least restrictive environment. If their needs could be met in a regular class, then that's where they were to be placed. Unfortunately, inclusion has turned into the haphazard dumping of children into classes for the purpose of complying with the law, rather than locating the best learning situation. Many "regular" classes were not designed for "regular" students, much less for those with special education needs. How did we serve these very wonderful children? We simply turned the system inside out. All children entered as children without pre-conceived notions. We utilized the Individual Educational Plan as a working, legal document, and then began the process of grouping students within their teams based on their particular learning needs. If the plan called for a self-contained setting at times, a small group devised from the team became that self-contained setting. If it called for a specific teaching style, the team members determined how to accomplish that goal. When this attention is given to children with special education needs and this amount of flexibility made available to all teachers, these students will be well served, and a school will never be out of compliance with federal or state laws.

1. Ensure that all children come to school simply as children.
   - Have no designated special education classrooms or wings.
   - Education professionals must know whom they are to serve and serve them appropriately.
   - Do not publicly identify students.
   - Respect the confidentiality of students at all times.
2. Do not label teachers assigned to special education students publicly as special education teachers. They are simply teachers.
   - The special education teacher will focus strongly on the special education students' Individual Education Plan.
   - All teachers are equal team members, sharing information, while focusing on the needs of all students.
3. Ensure the least restrictive environment.
   - The two classroom teachers, along with the special education teacher and educational assistant, are all equally considered teachers.
   - Teachers work with small groups, as students are divided based on the needs of the students and the activities they are doing.
   - Teachers may keep students in larger groups with added supervision when appropriate.
   - The special education teacher ensures that students with special needs are in the appropriate group.
     — Groups can be full-inclusion to self-contained as needed.
     — Students' roles in the group are monitored.
     — Flexibility is the key.
   - Community experiences with self-contained or mixed groups are designed to include students with special education needs.
4. Ensure an appropriate, active curriculum for all students. Then, and only then, will all children be served appropriately, and all students will fit into the regular class environment.
   - When utilized appropriately, projects provide for a whole range of abilities.
   - Community experiences provide a sense of reality to any lesson.
   - Demonstrations of learning show what students know.
   - Maintain the joy of learning. Learning is naturally exciting.
   - Make failure a learning experience, not a devastating experience.

With these four steps in place, all students will have a program designed with the flexibility to meet their individual needs. All students are included from the beginning and are then grouped for appropriate placement. Learning is real and is found everywhere students can put their hands on it.

Children must come to school as children, not branded as failures as soon as they enter the building.

THE ABSURDITY OF GRADES

As parents invade the secret world of education, they wonder how their children are progressing and what they are learning. When they look at their child's report card, they are ecstatic when they see an A and upset when they see a U or an F. Ingrained in the educational culture of the time, this system of progress reporting leaves the lingering question, What did my child learn? What does this archaic reporting system really tell parents about the progress of their child, and what does it hide from them? It tells them whether their child is performing better or worse than the student sitting next to him or her on a given day. Parents are led to believe that an A means their child is smart; a B means he or she is kind of smart; a C means average; a D means kind of stupid; and an F or U means the child is stupid. Ask any parent, or for that matter any child, and you will receive some variation of these definitions. But nowhere do grades tell what a child has learned.

Upon closer examination of parent conferences, a presentation of statistical information justifies and verifies that ominous letter grade. Averaging the scores on a range of chapter tests gives a grade explanation that is hard to argue with. Often, basing this data on a bell-shaped curve ensures that a significant number of students are kind of stupid or stupid. If that becomes politically incorrect, the bell-shaped curve is tilted a little, the chapter tests are dumbed down, and everyone is happy. Comparing students to each other brings up a concern about the significance of what average really is, about whether the bell-shaped curve is based on local data, state data, national data, or the opinion of some textbook company. These standards vary from state to state, from school to school, and yes, even from classroom to classroom. What is "kind of stupid" in one classroom may be "kind of smart" in another.

With the cloud of secrecy maintained, the focus is effectively taken off learning and placed directly on feel-good letter grades. When students muddle through with a D–, their skills remain flatlined, while the standards increase with the grade level. The result is children trying to read an eighth-grade standardized test with second-grade reading skills. This is clearly one reason why children don't learn how to read. Every day they become further and further behind, until they give up.

The teacher's focus on letter grades is yet another concern. It becomes more important for a child to increase his or her grade point average than to increase learning. This emphasis on statistics often has the teacher focused on chapter tests, percentages, and standardized bubble sheets to the point where they don't even have time to truly assess children and follow their real progress. With the addition of more and more standardized tests and the distraction of letter grades, teachers' focus moves further and further away from learning. My (EL's) recent conversation with a middle school teacher found her pointing to a whole cabinet full of creative activity plans she said she didn't have time to teach. She was required to teach to the standardized bubble test and use antiquated letter grades; thus, every ounce of her creative teaching time was swallowed up. This teacher is no longer in that school system. When we take away a teacher's ability to teach creatively, we either lose the teacher or, quite often, find that teachers revert to the dull drab classes of the past. Good teachers are lost, children are still failing, and the question regarding students still remains, What have they learned?

The flow of education is stopped when students who don't get it the first time around are forgotten, while their class moves on to the next chapter. Students, judged by a chapter test at the end of a six-week period, are forced to carry a label ranging from "stupid" to "smart" until the next six-week session is completed, with minimal chance to learn what they've missed. Of course, those students left behind can learn the missed material if they fail the whole year, go back to the beginning, and take everything over again. Facing the other alternative is just as devastating, especially in the area of mathematics, which is progressive. Through the dumbing-down process or statistical maneuvering, students somehow develop percentages that add up to a D, never again see the lesson, then move on to the next grade, falling further behind. This cycle of devastating failure might very well be the most notable reason for high dropout rates today.

Not only do letter grades damage those who fall behind, they have a negative affect on the A students also. These students may never reach their true potential, allowed to float through school without ever being challenged. The purpose of assessment is to guide the lesson plan, and those students who don't get anything wrong on a test provide minimal information to the teacher as to how to proceed. They can then float through school, regurgitating information they already know or can easily find out. These students, like all others, must be challenged. Everyone should miss some questions or fail at an experiment to ensure that he or she is challenged to learn. A students must be able to show what they cannot yet do, without the punishment of bad grades. They must be able to expand their minds to the fullest, not be told, "Okay, you're smart enough."

So many believe that if there is competition in real life, then there should be competition in school. If there are winners and losers in real life, then it only seems logical that there are winners and losers in school. We agree that there is competition in real life, and there are definitely winners and losers in real life. But remember, education is education; it is a means to an end, not the end itself. So, if we practice competition, that's okay. There will be winners and losers, but let's do it on the football field where the most that children can lose is a game. We can compete in debate, where the most they can lose is a meet, or in a spelling bee. This is healthy. But what do children have to lose when they compete for grades? They have their entire future to lose, and that's exactly what is happening. We are destroying many children when leaving children behind is part of the process. Only in writer Garrison Keillor's imaginary town, Lake Wobegon, is every child "above average." We are leaving so many behind when the dropout rate reaches 50 percent, as in urban areas. We are entrenched in a system where it is mathematically impossible for all children to succeed, and therein lies the fundamental problem. We must make dramatic change from that system to one where all children can succeed, a system where we are allowed to take all children from where they are and stay with them until they succeed. We must design a system where students compete against themselves, getting better and better every day, using time lines as guidelines for achievement, rather than deadlines for failure, a system where there are no losers and where we truly leave no child behind.

Anthony came to school just to mess around on a daily basis. He was horrible. One day he slowed down enough to have a heart-to-heart talk with his teacher, Samantha Powell. Ms. Powell told him that she had given up on him. There was no sense continuing her effort if nothing was going to be accomplished. In frustration, she asked him, "What do you want to learn?"

He replied, "I want to learn how to read."

She said, "Okay," and together they set up a computer program and other resources designed for Anthony to spend the whole day learning to read. He spent two solid weeks working on his reading with minimal disruption. The main issue was that he wanted to learn. He didn't want a grade because we didn't give grades. He simply wanted to learn, so he competed against himself, improved his skills, and felt good about it. He wasn't performing at "level" yet, but he gained skills and his chances of becoming proficient increased.

By detracting significantly from teachers' creativity, letter grades take away a wide variety of educational opportunities. One great way to teach writing is for parents and teachers to model it. My daughter's first attempts at a writing project elicited strong guidance from dad and mom. Her final product assuredly led to a good grade, but does that mean we were cheating? Of course it does, but only if letter grades are given. If they aren't given, there is no cheating, and parents and teachers can teach the way the children learn best, through modeling and working in small groups. There is no reason to cheat because the assessment now provides information valuable to the teacher and child without fear of failure. Without grades and unnecessary competition, the whole issue changes from playing the game of education to learning, and by cheating, there is no longer anything to be gained. The student is not a loser if he or she doesn't do well the first time; children can now be taught never to give up.

The purpose of assessment is to determine what children know and what they have to work on. A test, being a feeble form of assessment, is often given at the end of a chapter. Logic tells you that you take what students miss and reteach it. In reality, once a test is complete, teachers move on to the next chapter. Those teachers fail as teachers.

Remember Sunny, the new student who initially showed absolutely no desire to join the reading group? He gained dramatically in reading levels in two short years. This accomplishment underlines the basic philosophy of MVS. Sunny transferred to our school after making no gains in reading for six straight years. If we had given him the grades he "deserved" during his first six-week period with us, he would have failed. It took him more than six weeks to "buy into" our staff. After he had failed consistently for six years, we would have certainly lost him if we'd graded him accurately, but if we had given him a C to boost his self-esteem, he would have continued to fail. Perceiving our lowered expectations of him, he would have seen no reason to achieve. No matter what letter grade he was given, it would have proven destructive. So we gave him, like all other students at MVS, no letter grades and took him from where he was, celebrating his successes along the way. We told him and his parents what he was learning. No wonder students drop out before tenth grade in the old system; they don't have a chance. They are told they are stupid year after year, and they begin to believe it. Grades merely end up serving as a smokescreen and ensure that parents know nothing about what their child has learned.

The change away from letter grades is especially difficult since they are so ingrained in the minds of parents. "We had letter grades when we were in school, and we turned out okay." First, not everyone turned out okay. Just look at the number of people their age who are in jail. Second, this is a new day, a day when everyone has to achieve to succeed. How do we get this grade-free concept across? How do we convince parents to abandon this historic way of viewing their children's educational achievement? We face parents and explain, one parent at a time. There we were in our second year under the no-grade system, when a new parent, Ms. Madison, came in with her son James to talk to us about reading. We shared with her the results of a reading assessment that showed her son was reading at around the third-grade level. We knew the levels were not completely accurate, and we explained that this was just a snapshot to give us an idea of where to start. We also observed his reading abilities in the classroom with a similar conclusion. Ms. Madison was livid.

"How can he be at the third-grade level when last year he got a C in a sixth-grade English course at his other school? How could my child lose ground at your school? What kind of school do you have here?"

"How well do you think James reads?" we asked.

"Well," she said, "he doesn't read too well."

"We will teach him 'from where he is' rather than pretending that he is on level," we responded. "We will verify his learning and allow him to progress at his fastest speed. This way we know we will see progress."

The reality was that the C given him previously was misinforming. It did not tell James or his mother what he had learned, nor did it tell him what he needed to learn. Grading systems had been substantially dumbed down to allow for a feel-good grade. We promised results. We used the checklist and growth charts to tell the parent the truth about what his or her child was learning and how hard he or she was working. Eventually, this was well accepted and appreciated by parents. Finally, they knew they were given accurate information.

Elimination of letter grades by itself does not accomplish anything. They must be replaced by authentic assessments of learning to which students are held accountable. Our proficiency lists and growth charts tell the story.

SQUASHING THE STANDARDISTOS

The assessment of students is only as good as the information obtained and the application of it to their needs. Entrenched in the present system is an assessment process that does neither. Current standards are designed mainly around multiple-choice tests to determine whether students are adequate with the no. 2 pencil and bubble sheet. The memory of being herded like cattle into a sterile room with a proctor dictating rules in a monotone voice causes adults to shudder years later. Imagine how children feel. Who does well on this type of test?

Recently a local radio station in Milwaukee, Wisconsin, offered such a test to some of its radio personalities. They admitted they were nervous as they began this dastardly assignment. When they received the results, according to a discussion on their afternoon show, one scored well above the others. His response, as relayed by that program, was that he had always been good at taking this kind of test. All students are not equal in their ability to take these tests under these conditions. What is the best way to assess children? Make the assessment authentic through a demonstration of learning, such as projects, presentations, hands-on activities, or individual attention. These assessments take away the roadblocks and allow children to demonstrate learning in the way they do it best.

There are many ways to ensure an accurate assessment, but how then is it applied to the needs of the students? After all the effort, energy, and money spent on bubble tests, the result leaves simply a dot on a chart that reveals nothing to educators, parents, or to the students themselves about what students have learned or need to learn. Dictated by the state, meaning the federal government in this case, with little concern for the community, standardized tests are imposed on students in a manner similar to that of the communist countries. In the 1950s, the state saw the need to increase mathematics scores to compete with the Soviet Union and raised the standards. When this happened, they made job-specific skills required for all students, regardless of their interests. If the quest is to ensure job-specific high math standards for the legal profession, for example, should we expect mathematicians to be adept at presenting a defense case? No, you say? You say you don't want to learn law; you want to be a mathematician. Exactly, I say, and some people aren't interested in being mathematicians either. Even though everyone should receive some math, to continue teaching it on a job-specific level is extreme. Even though it is valuable to introduce students to those job-specific skills, do so without the threat of failure and not as required proficiencies. High standards, those that are at the job-specific level, force students into areas of study regardless of their interests. When is the last time you used the quadratic equation?

We must not continue to fail students because they aren't interested in learning something they will never need to know anyway.

Significant information must be made available to students and parents to allow them to choose areas of study of interest to them. The highest level of learning must then be made available in those areas to allow students to learn and learn until they reach the stars, and then learn some more. Isn't that better than the state picking their area for them or some guidance counselor counseling them into an area they think the child will want. Think about the possibilities of having higher-level clubs for the purpose of introducing all children to these skills, so they may determine where their interests lie, clubs where they don't have to worry about time frames or failure or grades. Imagine how many more children would take the leap into that area as a profession, and how many more children will then go to college. We cannot continue to scare children away from college with the threat of massive failure and rigid time lines.

This does not mean that higher-level, job-specific skills should not be taught. As a matter of fact, a broader base of these skills should be experienced by all and taught to those who choose to learn them.

When we abandon standards as we know them, the concept of proficiencies is introduced on a whole new level. Our concept of proficiencies has the following qualities:

- Proficiencies are real, usable needs of all students and are not job specific. See the section titled "Charting the Course," above, for examples.
- Our time lines are guidelines for learning, rather than deadlines for failure. Children will achieve, some sooner, some later.
- Proficiencies do not entail one high-stakes test, but many assessments throughout the student's school years and a final presentation.
- Proficiencies are demonstrations of learning, assessed in many ways, not just by multiple-choice tests and not limited by the scope of a paper-and-pencil test. Children demonstrate learning by using all of their senses.
- Criteria for proficiencies are developed locally with input from parents, community members, educators, and, yes, even politicians.

These are reviewed and adapted every year, allowing parents to drive the direction of their child's learning.

An example of the failure of standards is the concept of algebra for all. Often taught as simply a matter of plugging in the numbers, the true concept of algebra as a thought process is often lost. In addition, it is clear that not all students learn a process in the same way. As a thought process, is algebra different from logic? Dr. Howard Gardner states in *Frames of Mind*, "Logic and mathematics have had different histories but, in modern times, have moved closer together" (p. 135). Some experts have stated that algebra and logic have moved so close that the two have become one. When we understand that students learn in different ways, isn't it wise that those who learn best by words should then learn by words?

> *Give children the power to learn. They can memorize when you tell them, but they will only learn when they are ready. They still control their own minds, and they will open them or close them based on their perception of the value of the incoming information.*

WHAT IS A GOOD SCHOOL? WHAT IS A BAD SCHOOL?

Local, state, and federal officials have paid lip service to the concept of closing failed schools as the first step toward the success of public schools. Presidential candidates and other politicians shout it to the masses to capture their votes, but do they know the damage they are doing, and do they even know what constitutes a failed school? When the extreme pressure of schools winning or losing pits educators against each other, the students become the victims.

ACT NOW 2003, a student advocacy group, tells the Steve Orel story. In spring 2000, Birmingham, Alabama, adult-education instructor Steve Orel noticed that students terminated by local high schools were enrolling in his GED program. After an investigation initiated by a school board member, Orel learned that 522 students had received the same "push out" papers. The official reason for all the students' dismissal was "Withdrawn: lack of interest." Orel wondered how much lack of interest there could be when the students were trying to get into his educational program. He discovered that schools had been threatened with state takeover if they didn't raise scores. He also learned that the superintendent's bonus depended on his ability to raise standardized test scores. Orel and others concluded that to raise scores the school district got rid of low scorers. Steve Orel's whistle-blowing cost him his job.

We must also take a whole new look at how we assess schools; no longer can we simply turn to averages, standards, and letter grades to guide us. Currently, the federal government uses the average of standardized test scores as a factor in determining a failed school. Assessment becomes especially difficult for those schools, especially urban schools, with high mobility rates. Averages frequently end up being based on students the schools don't even have. For example, standardized tests are given once a year. If the test is given in May, those students who enrolled in one school in April are part of that school's year-end average, even though they just relocated and were educated for eight months or longer at another school. Those relocating and leaving one school before the May standardized test are not included at all in that school's year-end data; they are part of a year-end average in another school, even though the school they left serviced them for eight months. Clearly, this is one of many reasons why the single annual standardized test is not a valid way to assess schools.

Assessment can be done many ways, such as with a portfolio, a project, or a presentation evaluated by a teacher or a team, or even by a snapshot test, if it's used right. First, assessments must be conducted at the local level and must give good feedback to teachers. Second, to ensure that all students receive pre- and postassessments to record their gains accurately, assessments must be given when students enter the school and before they leave the school during a particular year. This keeps assessment within the time frame that the school has responsibility for a child. Using standards as a guideline only, student progress is the ultimate focus. When used as a rigid time line, standards for schools are only effective if all students start in the same place. Reality suggests, however, that students rarely start at the same place.

Again, we talk about Sunny. According to our snapshot assessment, he was reading on 4.5-grade level when he neared the end of his middle school years at MVS. According to existing standards, this was a failed student and a failed school. But Sunny had come to the school two years previous reading on the preprimer level and wouldn't even attempt reading. After learning nothing in the previous six years, he had advanced 4.5 grade levels in reading in two years, and more importantly, he had discovered the joy of reading. Is this still a failed school? By federal government standards it is.

An honest assessment of student progress within a school is only one of many factors that show which schools are succeeding and which are failing. It must, however, be an honest assessment that gives real indicators as to how much impact school educators have on individual students. When assessment shows individual growth, those schools that take on the challenge of all children, especially in urban areas, will no longer automatically be labeled as bad schools. They will be considered for their progress, not based on an average, but based on the number of individuals who show gain. For example, 48 percent of students gained significantly in reading skills, 30 percent made their yearly gains, and 22 percent showed no gains. This tells how the school does with each student it serves. Used as a guideline however, this student assessment model is only one small portion of the overall judgment of a school's quality.

How should schools be judged? What assurance is there that a school is doing its job? One must take a look at a variety of indicators, starting with asking parents' opinions. Surveys sent and given to parents on a regular basis allow for regular input. They keep parents informed and serve as a guide to their view of the success of the school. Parents are, after all, the key stakeholders in their children's education, and as such, should be the key players in evaluating the schools.

Essential to MVS's assessment concept was the ongoing survey of parents. Continued feedback, necessary to understand truly the feelings of all parents, allowed for balanced and informed opinions. It was of utmost importance to discover the feelings and attitudes of those parents who had minimal or no contact with the school. Their opinions were equally important to us, so we went out after them, even if getting a response to a survey took a knock on their door or a visit to their job. Large surveys sent to parents on a yearly basis are seldom given deep thought and are answered by few. It is important to remember students and staff members in this process. An ongoing honest survey of students' and staff members' attitudes and opinions is essential to the success and appropriate assessment of a school. Determine what is important to your school at a local level, and get input from all stakeholders.

- Student goals and objectives should be observed.
  — Academic progress in subject areas is noted, with standards as guidelines.
  — Demonstrations of knowledge, skills, and abilities are acknowledged.
- Student attendance often demonstrates the child's comfort at and the students' valuing of the school.
  — Awareness of reasons for absenteeism helps paint a clearer picture.
  — Truancy is unacceptable. Although parents are the main players in this issue, the school has a responsibility to provide an environment conducive to learning.
- Attitudes of all stakeholders paint a clear picture of the success of the school.
  — Parent surveys are an important part of the acceptance of an educational endeavor.
  — Staff surveys reflect the workability of various theories and ideas.
  — Student surveys will show their opinions and their comfort in the learning atmosphere.
  — Community surveys give a broad sense of a school's success.
- Long-term successes of students are an indicator of school quality.
  — Track and survey former students for a specific length of time.
  — Visitations and presentations by former students should be arranged.
- Input measures such as school-design changes indicate an effort to make successful changes to meet today's needs.
  — Determine the effectiveness of the educational delivery systems of education.
  — Determine if the school is run in a cost-effective manner.

When developing your school's assessment, do not look at averages or standards because they do not give you information about the students you have served. Use a wide variety of indicators.

CHAPTER 5

Together in the Community

Many education experts pay lip service to the value of neighborhood schools, but few seem to grasp the reality of what they mean. A neighborhood school is a place students and parents can easily access without driving across town or changing buses three or four times. It's a place to which they can walk and where meetings of parents are also meetings of neighbors. In the name of other social and academic objectives, the desegregation order of the 1960s and the magnet school concept of more recent times have left most urban systems with no real neighborhood middle schools. Putting the community-education philosophy at the core brings the school close to the community and the community close to the school. This is practical as well as philosophical. After all, educating children at their most vulnerable stage of development is hard enough without removing the much-needed resources of the community. Not just a slogan, the African proverb, "it takes a whole village to raise a child," means seeing school, family, and community not as separate entities, but as a team, working together to support the educational development of children. It means that children go out into the community and that community members come into the school. When a school becomes the hub of the community, it contains services for all community members: a senior center, an adult-education center, medical services, a clothing exchange, a day care, a medical clinic, and much more, right there in the school.

> *The whole-village concept is a support system with parents at the forefront. They are the child's first and best teachers.*

BRINGING IN THE PARENTS

Parents, as the guiding lights of a school designed for children, must no longer take a back seat in the educational direction of the school. All too often, parent committees and organizations are used as a smokescreen to stifle real parent involvement. Scripted meetings are the order of the day, designed to hold parents at bay, while the real agendas are determined from behind closed doors. We started MVS by welcoming all parents for information sessions that allow true parent feedback.

On a warm summer's evening in mid-August, we watched parents approaching the school from blocks away. What a wonderful sight, parents walking to their neighborhood middle school on a beautiful summer evening. We had sent flyers, called parents, and promised some good hot snacks, hoping for a decent turnout to hear us present our plans for the new, innovative MVS. Families started showing up slowly and continued until we had a full house. This was the students' first time in the school, so teachers Roxane, Samantha, and Trina took them into another room to prepare for a small presentation, while we discussed our unique ideas with a quite receptive group of parents. As a part of the meeting, the children helped us with a "cookie assessment" presentation that we had learned at Alverno College. The students were given three kinds of cookies to assess, with one group giving letter grades and another giving a short description. The first cookie was given an A by the first team. Everyone tried to guess what kind it was, but they didn't have a clue. The second team was to give a short description of the item.

"My cookie is small and round and made of sugar and dough with pieces of chocolate in it," said Angela.

Hmmmmmm, could it be a chocolate chip cookie? Everyone, of course, guessed right.

"At the Village, we will tell you what your child has learned and we won't hide behind a letter grade. Like the cookie, we want parents to know what their child has learned," I (EL) said. Everyone enjoyed the evening, and a strong partnership with parents was begun.

Keep parents on board with the philosophy. Remember, they can walk to the school.

Parent involvement in the daily routine of the school is an integral part of their child's education. Welcomed to witness firsthand everyday events, parents were encouraged to volunteer in the classroom, wherever that classroom happened to be at the time. A school's need for chaperones drives volunteerism in most schools, but our philosophy was to throw open the doors to involve parents at any time throughout the year.

For our first community experience, we sent out an invitation to all parents to join our students and staff at a cultural music and dance program at the Milwaukee High School of the Arts. Loading the students and staff onto the bus, I (MGB) did a double take as I noticed a woman in short shorts smoking a cigarette; she appeared to be the mother of one of our students. I approached her and asked if she was going to join us. She said, "Yes, and I'm happy to be invited." Upon being informed of the no-smoking policy, she joined students and staff as the excursion headed toward its destination. Parents were encouraged to simply enjoy the presentation and learn from it. No duties were given them. That day was a wonderful example of learning outside the four classroom walls. Students had been well prepared for the activity, and they followed up with a roundtable discussion. Excited about the activity, the same mom stated, "I had a fabulous time. Would it be okay if I come back again for tomorrow's trip?"

I said, "Of course, but please wear shorts that are a tiny bit longer." Mom showed up very well dressed for her second trip, bringing her sister and her best friend from the neighborhood with her three little kids. She said, "I had such a great time yesterday, that I just had to come today and bring my friends." They all boarded the bus, and from that day on, that mom was one of our greatest supporters. Contrary to the tradition of snubbing parents and neighbors, when you say parents are welcome, mean it. Every trip is simply an extension of the classroom, and the classroom must be a friendly place for parents wherever it happens to be.

Parents are not only customers; they are assets to every lesson.

DO YOU KNOW YOUR NEIGHBOR?

When community schools ceased to exist, an important function of neighborliness was removed. Remember the good old days when if a child did something wrong several blocks from home, someone would call that child's parent and that child would be dealt with. Neighbors trusted neighbors to help. When children started traveling great distances to a variety of different schools, away from their homes and neighbors, this familiarity was lost. The school was no longer the meeting place for parents; thus, neighbors didn't know their neighbors anymore. Without familiarity came mistrust; with mistrust came the loss of support needed to understand fully what your children were doing when they were away from you.

That this lack of familiarity and trust is a major cause of discipline problems became apparent the day Tanya and Wanda came to school ready to demolish each other. The shouting stopped and the fists flew as soon as I (EL) reached the scene, revealing once again the principle that kids are more likely to fight when someone shows up to stop them. With some help, I got a brutal situation under control. The girls were suspended and sent home separately to avoid further trouble. We thought we had a day to figure things out, but an hour later Tanya appeared with a group of people she described as relatives. I counted six extra people and was convinced they weren't there just to talk. Just as I convinced them that the other student wasn't at school and they should go home, Wanda arrived with her group. In the middle of a very threatening situation, I wanted to call home to verify if my life insurance policy was current. After what seemed like weeks, I got them to agree to a conference with one child and one parent on each side. Everyone else left.

At the conference, they talked and I mediated for close to two hours. During this time, we uncovered valuable information. The fact that the whole difficulty was based on "he say, she say" became trivial in the face of the knowledge that these parents were neighbors, living just two blocks from each other, and they had never met. As the discussion continued, they found many things in common, and they began to trust each other. The conference, which began with threats and shouting, ended with tears, hugs, and an exchange of phone numbers. The conference happened quite simply because both families had easy access to the school.

In the neighborhood, the door to communication is just a short walk away, at the school. Neighborhood schools once again become a meeting place for neighbors and, when communication between them increases, the chance of their children causing trouble "down the street" decreases. Parents begin to look out for each other's children, and if rumors start, they just pick up the phone. When the child gets home, the parents are waiting at the door for them. I think we all remember situations like that, and being busted was bone chilling, as it should be.

It is a truism to say that schools must be in close touch with the parents of their students. This concept, neglected as children move out of elementary school, highlights the importance of parents' talking to each other and working together for the good of the child before a crisis happens. A neighborhood school's doors must be open to parents to meet school staff, as well as for them to meet their neighbors to provide a vehicle for communication and neighborhood team building. Trust building between parents and teachers must be an integral part of a school philosophy. Because they remain with the same students for the full three years, teachers and parents are able to develop a strong rapport. Adding to this, the close proximity of students' homes and the presence of phones in every classroom make home communication a top priority.

ALL PARENTS TAKING CHARGE OF THEIR CHILDREN'S EDUCATIONAL LIVES

Key to the operation of a school is allowing all stakeholders to take charge of the educational lives of children. In an era when more and more parents find themselves isolated from the school, our goal is that all stakeholders become planners and facilitators. Rarely do educators fully understand the necessity of allowing this to happen. Charged with making decisions on behalf of the larger group, administrators or a small number of parents and community members in a council are usually in control, with grassroots parents too often isolated from this process. Their opinions must be heard. Parents should be brought into the process in a way that is appropriate and valuable. It is evident that parents do not, in general, have the expertise to develop classroom strategies, and students don't have the skills necessary to hire or fire teachers. It is also important, under the Village philosophy, that teachers have the greatest voice in developing classroom strategies, while parents have the strongest voice in the overall goals of the school.

Clarifying a major misunderstanding commonly held by educators, separate roles for parents and community members are designated, maintaining the sacred role of parents as the primary stakeholder. Community members play a supportive, rather than a decision-making, role. Collaboration with a wide range of businesses and community agencies must play an integral part in a school's philosophy and is a helpful tool in promoting the educational development of children. We must never lose sight of the reality that the customer is the parent. A unique concept is that, under the Village philosophy, stakeholders do not necessarily have an equal voice in each of the subparts of the school's operations. Decisions are made by those who are most affected by them. The difficulty is determining to what extent the educational plan affects each of the stakeholders. To resolve this issue, the school council looks to the Parity Decision-Making Model designed by Dr. Ed Pino (see table 5.1).

As we seek an effective way to bring parents into the process, we look to politicians who continuously survey their constituents to keep their fingers on the pulse. Regular parent surveys ensure that all voices are heard and all stakeholders are welcomed into the decision-making process. We found the most effective surveys utilized an automated phone machine, as well as paper surveys mailed home on a regular basis. The surveys were short, with no more than four or five questions, thus allowing parents to focus on the subject matter. The old administrative trick of hiding an issue in the middle of a huge survey was not conducive to parent input; rather, it confused parents, distancing them from the school.

Of utmost importance is to truly use the surveys. Parents, for example, might choose the starting time for the school or select the

Table 5.1 Sample Parity Table Application
(Prepared for the Milwaukee Village School and Community Center Proposal)

Participating Partners	Goals	Program Objectives	Facilities	Personnel	Curriculum	Instructional Strategies	Staff Development	Funding	Accountability	Communication
Students	20	15	10	10	20	10	10	10	20	10
Staff	10	30	20	20	40	60	30	10	20	10
Principal	10	25	30	50	20	10	40	40	20	20
Parents	50	15	20	10	10	10	10	20	20	40
Community	10	15	20	10	10	10	10	20	20	20
Totals	100	100	100	100	100	100	100	100	100	100

Based on Ed Pino's Parity Decision-Making Model © 1993, Edward C. Pino.

school calendar. Curriculum, while mainly in the hands of educators, may take a focus recommended by parents, such as putting an emphasis on foreign language or the arts. These are real decisions made by real parents after they are fully informed. Implementing the survey concept will take time, but the more parents see their ideas used, the more surveys will be returned. Never again will parents be manipulated into agreeing with already stated ideas or scripted council meetings. As our guiding lights, the parents are full partners welcomed into the education process.

Milwaukee Village School Parent Survey

1. Next school year we will be able to add one additional elective class. What subject would you like to have added to our school?
   _____ Drama
   _____ Dance
   _____ Foreign Language
   _____ Other _____

2. Do you want to combine with the high school and be one school serving grades six through twelve?
   _____ Yes   _____ No

3. Currently school starts at 8:20 A.M. The high school students start at 8:30 A.M. What time would you like school to start?
   _____ Stay at 8:20 A.M.
   _____ Start at 8:30 A.M. with the high school students
   _____ Start at 8:00 A.M.
   _____ Other _____

4. Do you want your child released at the end of the day at the same time high school students are released?
   _____ Yes   _____ No

Every one of these questions was asked and parents' preferences were implemented.

For question 1, 69 percent requested a foreign language, and the school added a foreign language to its choice of classes. We started with Swahili and later added Spanish.

For question 2, 100 percent answered no, and we did not combine with the high school.

For question 3, 87 percent requested that the school start at 8:00 A.M. For question 4, 100 percent requested that Village students not be released at the same time that high school students were.

No longer do the parents involved consist of four or five parents. All parents must be heard.

SAFE PASSAGE

Concern about the health and welfare of their children has caused many parents to believe it is safer to put them onto a school bus than it is for children to walk to a neighborhood school. Middle school administrators responsible for transportation know better, but all parents' concerns must be addressed. Utilizing community and parent resources, a "safe passage" philosophy is designed to support children on their way to and from school.

Utilizing the resources of the whole village, a strong and secure plan is essential to maintaining the school as a safe haven. The following are steps toward implementing a safe passage at your school:

1. Place a city map on a corkboard with pins that indicate where every student lives.
2. Designate a minimum number of main routes for students to walk to and from their homes. Main streets with good visibility are recommended.
3. Garner the support of the local district police department to patrol these routes, as often as possible, especially during student release time.
4. Utilize all resources currently available.
    a. Alert all elementary school crossing guards to support middle school students walking in their area.
    b. Get support from parent volunteers to patrol certain areas that are determined to be trouble spots.
    c. Visit businesses along the routes to solicit their support to watch out for the children.
    d. Ask neighbors to step out on their porch and keep an eye out during dismissal time.

e. Delegate a staff member to drive the routes to ensure safety for the students.

Yes, this is a whole-village effort. All stakeholders are involved.

The more eyes there are in the neighborhood, the safer the neighborhood becomes.

GETTING TO KNOW THE NEIGHBORHOOD

We begin our venture into the community right at our doorstep; after all, the best resources are those most easily accessed. How did we find out what was available right there in the neighborhood shared by school and home? Just like we always did. We put the children at the forefront, and they proceeded to discover their neighbors. The assignment was to map the neighborhood. Not only were they to diagram the streets, they were to identify any and all businesses and organizations in the area. After charting the streets around the school, the students came upon a day care in need of beautification. Later, this became Wanita's day care as she took on the challenge as her pet project. This was one way we got our business partners. Neighbors began to recognize the children, and the children began to connect with neighbors they had never met before.

When the community blends with the school, doors open wide for a whole range of experiences and opportunities. On one such occasion, students were involved in a thematic unit on nutrition.

Student representatives from each classroom were chosen by their peers to attend student-conducted meetings for the purpose of planning an intergenerational food project. Elderly people in their community were invited to enjoy a series of lunches planned by students with a strong focus on good nutrition. The elderly neighbors were transported to school for ten days of lunches, with the initial ones designed not only to acquaint the visitors with the students, but to dispel the myth held by some that the school and the children were "bad." A positive environment within the school immediately allowed children to accomplish these goals quickly. Good food and good conversation were the order of the day, while Mr. Johnson, a neighbor, taught us about a "walking plate."

"This food was so wonderful," he said, "I would like a 'walking plate' to go home with me."

"What's a walking plate?" asked Prince.

"A full plate of good food that I can take home with me," replied Mr. Johnson.

So from that time on, at the end of each luncheon, the students prepared walking plates for each guest to take home.

As they became more acquainted with their elderly neighbors, students took the next step to determine what other services they could offer their newfound friends. The focus was to find out what the people needed, rather than tell them, "This is what I am going to do for you." Requests came in as neighbors requested assistance with a variety of tasks, from planting shrubs and grass to cleaning up yards and alleys.

Once students clearly understood how they could assist the elderly in their community, they decided on the assignments for each project. These miniprojects were developed and accomplished through collaboration with parents, teachers, students, the school psychologist, and the administrator, as well as community businesses. These individuals weren't just the neighbors around the school; they were also the neighbors of the children.

As the students moved forward on their projects, they followed a process:

1. Determine what materials and person-power would be needed to complete each identified task.
2. Determine how much financial support each project would need.
3. Develop an action plan to ensure project completion in a cost-effective manner.
4. Set up accounts with local businesses.
5. Shop for needed supplies.
6. Identify the best time frame in which to complete each task and job assignment.

Interaction with and support from local businesses was essential to our philosophy. A special emphasis was placed on those businesses in close proximity to the home and school neighborhood, as well as those that were African American owned and operated. Empowerment of children also led to some unusual situations. Imagine being a clerk at a hardware store when fifteen middle school students climb out of a van with a shopping list in hand and no money. The student spokesman, Paul, made a request to open an account. The confused clerk took Paul and two other students back to see the manager, while the teacher remained unnoticed in the back of the store. After a short discussion, Paul came out and announced that they had to return to school to get a letter of authorization from the administrator. The students hopped back into the van and were driven back to school. Ten minutes after informing the administrator of their need, Paul and all fifteen students were back in the van, letter in hand, off once again to the hardware store. Paul returned to the manager with the authorization letter and proceeded to open an account. What a wonderful lesson was shared by all, and the professionalism of the store personnel was commendable. It was definitely a teachable moment.

Comparative shopping was the order of the day as the students compared hammers, saws, rakes, and a whole range of tools needed to complete their neighborhood tasks. With sufficient supplies in hand, the student leaders returned to their respective classrooms to garner more workers for their projects. Working as a team to complete each item on their list, their one goal was to fulfill the dreams and wishes of their elderly recipients.

One elderly woman had requested that her yard be cleaned, bushes trimmed, and trash collected from the alley. Students worked diligently, filled many, many large trash bags, and readied them for disposal. Then, she said she sure would like a few flowers to brighten up the yard. She left town for a few days, and when she returned, her son stated that "tears welled up in her eyes" when she saw her beautiful yard resplendent with many colorful flowers. Another woman wanted rose bushes planted in her yard; another needed grass planted in the front of her house; and an elderly man needed help cleaning up his yard. More and more flowers were needed, and students were adamant about purchasing them in the neighborhood or at least from a black-owned business. Van driver David Crouthers suggested they take a ride to check out a greenhouse he knew about. David was the African American owner of D&L Bus Company and was a full partner in many of our ventures.

When the van pulled up to the greenhouse, fifteen middle school students bounded out and were met at the door by a woman who, not seeing the teacher, would not allow them into the business. I (MGB) asked to see the manager, and what happened next was a partnership made in heaven. Out of the back area came a very, very tall African American man who extended a very, very large hand. I started looking at his very, very large feet and continued up to the top of his head. I stood at about his belt line. We grasped hands, and I looked into his eyes.

"My students would like to shop for flowers, but I do not have any money with me at this time."

He said, "Bring them in. Let them have whatever they need."

I went on to explain that I did have money in a school account and would pay the bill as soon as I could turn in the receipt. Will Allen, the owner, said that would not be a problem and turned us loose. The students were ecstatic about the wide array of flowers to choose from and loaded many flats into the van. We were off to beautify Ms. Starnes's home.

It was so wonderful to see these students planning, calling, making arrangements, and then carrying out their projects in the community. Wanita's project was at Grandma's Day Care. Her crew was assigned to clean up the lot, then plant flowers and vegetables. Curtis Lawrence, a reporter for the *Milwaukee Journal-Sentinel*, joined the students at this site. He came dressed in a suit and tie. Antoine, a student, informed him that he had better get comfortable and grab a rake "because no one just stands around!" In a few minutes, he took off the suit jacket and loosened his tie. The next day, a wonderful article appeared in the newspaper. The students were thrilled, and many in the community were amazed at just what these young people were able to accomplish and how much they had learned about organic gardening. Parents were extremely pleased with their children and happy that they brought vegetables home to eat and to plant.

During this whole process, students measured, managed money, wrote and read instructions, and made oral presentations about their activities to others. Especially significant, they gained a greater understanding about their local environment and businesses. All integrated academics were consistent with their classroom goals and objectives, and they had real meaning for everyone.

HEADING FOR THE HILLS

Too often overlooked or entirely missing from an urban education, an exploration of the historical roots of these city kids can provide a whole range of new experiences and teachable moments.

After all, many grandparents and great-grandparents of urban children grew up on a farm or in a small rural community. A simple greenhouse will give children a taste of this country life, as well as a basic understanding of the value of good food. "A Farm City Link" was a project dedicated to positive growth that enhanced youth life skills, vocational opportunities, and community responsibility through organic agricultural education and experimental programs.

- Students, chosen by interviews, attended twenty-seven educational sessions.
- The greenhouse staff provided the seeds, containers, soil, and skills necessary for students to be successful.
- A professional farmer was the teacher at the greenhouse.
- Students became the teachers as they presented to their classmates back at school.
- When students returned home they shared their crops, while educating their parents, friends, and relatives.

Referring to the activity simply as the "gardening project," teachers enabled all students, regardless of their academic level, to learn by using a variety of approaches. At the same time, farmer Will Allen gave lessons in caring about others, giving back, appreciating what one is able to do, and sharing with the community. It was amazing to see the students work together as a group and learn via a hands-on nontraditional approach. The students learned about many different seeds and plants. They sowed, cultivated, transplanted, propagated, and nurtured their plants to maturity. They learned about giving, as they gave a portion of their produce to someone else. They learned about marketing a product, especially something they had grown. Our integrated curriculum included science, nutrition, character development, and community activities.

- Throughout the year, a photo album documented greenhouse activities.
- Videotapes were made and shared with other classrooms.
- Students kept journals and brought them to the greenhouse to add information.
- Students brought seedlings back to school to grow in their classrooms and share with their classmates and parents.

Culminating activities for the "gardening project" included a student-organized recognition ceremony at a Mexican restaurant, as well as the final report to the State of Wisconsin Branch and Grant Funding Agency. Both were very emotionally moving events. All final reports to the state, except one, were given by adults, and Prince wanted his presentation to be last. This 4' 10" young man rose to new heights when he delivered a knockout speech about his gardening project. Then, he proceeded to introduce Mr. Allen, a 6' 8" former professional basketball player, who told the audience that it had been his pleasure to give students more than just methodology and techniques to plant seed and grow a variety of plants. The project really gave the children a true sense of another way of life.

GET OUT OF THIS BUILDING! AND DON'T COME BACK UNTIL YOU'VE LEARNED SOMETHING

Critical to the school concept is taking students into the community to gain firsthand a wide range of educational experiences, and not just an occasional visit, but regular visits on an ongoing basis. Complicating this are teachers and parents alike who do not fully understand the concept. All too often field trips are associated with playtime and not considered truly educational. Mandate that all trips do the following:

- Relate to the overall educational plan
- Promote fundamental learning, including reading, writing, math and/or science, and speaking
- Include pretrip planning and research
- Include a posttrip wrap-up by all students, including presentations to other classes

The last insures that the children become the teachers, so others can gain from their experiences.

There is a vast array of real-life experiences to be gained exploring the neighborhood. Experiences in the community become an extension of the classroom, not play, and are certainly not used as reward or punishment. At MVS, students weren't excluded from a trip because they didn't "earn" it; the trips were the classroom. Does a child have to earn the right to be in the classroom if his or her homework isn't done? Certainly, they must complete all tasks, as well as behave, but the trips are not carrots to be dangled in front of children. Trips are an extension of the classroom and a great way for children to learn.

> *Historically, we have told children they must learn in the way in which they are least capable before we let them learn in the way they learn best. Think about it. All educational experiences and the classroom are one and the same.*

Overcoming the legal obstacles and complex scheduling to get students into the community has always been an administrative nightmare. First, it became necessary to streamline the cumbersome policy of having a parent sign a field-trip form for every activity. These trips were the classroom, and students shouldn't need special permission to go to their classroom. It was time to sit down with the legal eagles and come up with a plan that allowed for easier movement and assured the parents that their children were receiving a safe, quality education.

A community-experience form was developed for the full year, allowing students to access the community throughout the year. It recognized a "school without walls," where the classroom was everywhere. Parents were, of course, notified of all educational experiences, and administrative approval was necessary. The only limitation was that the activity must relate to the unit of study, and it must be educational.

Now that we have permission, how do we access the community with sufficient adult supervision? How do we ensure that all classes remaining in the school are covered? Traditionally, a wide variety of administrative adjustments have been required to ensure that all students receive proper supervision and adequate educational support. Teachers must be sought to cover classes and provide chaperones, students are pulled out of an array of classes, and the whole learning process is disrupted. Schools were clearly not designed for this to happen smoothly. Of course not; how far could you travel in the nineteenth century?

Large time blocks allowed education to control time frames, while teachers were able to alter schedules as needed. When a teacher wanted to take students into the community, all he or she had to do was plan with the team and go. And go they did. Learning, by nature, is fun. Monique Brown, a superb teacher and a natural for our philosophy, took her students on a walk to the neighborhood McDonald's about four blocks away. It was not simply a walk. First, they talked about houses and how to design a house, with a special emphasis on living space, design, and color. Charting the color of each house they passed, their first objective was to determine what the most popular color was in their neighborhood (math). They also paid attention to the design. All houses were basically rectangular, but in the classroom preactivity discussions, the class had determined that there seemed to be more available living space in a round house. On their walk, they discovered a construction crew in the neighborhood working on an office building. The students wanted to know why they were building a square building, when there seemed to be more usable space in a round building, so they simply stopped the construction workers and asked them. The workers complied and the students learned (job exploration). Back in the classroom, they designed their own houses, made models out of cardboard (art/design), wrote about them (writing), and presented their findings to classmates (speaking). No one ever told them they were learning geometry, charting, reading, writing, and speaking skills. Not everyone, however, necessarily learned the same things. Some learned geometry, but others weren't ready to comprehend it yet; they may have had goals to learn charting in the area of math, or, at the very least, were introduced to the concept of geometry. All had the opportunity to improve their writing skills, and all experienced the job the construction workers were doing. There was something for everyone to learn at his or her level, all from a simple trip to McDonald's. They remembered what they had learned because it was real, and they demonstrated what they had learned through their projects. Teacher Monique Brown kept a strong focus on what her students learned and was very aware of, and concerned for, those who didn't. She did not give up on them and move on to the next chapter and the next chapter test. She paid specific attention to them and had the flexibility to teach the skills again in a different way.

Learning, by nature, is fun, but it is not play. High expectations for students continue, and every educational minute has meaning.

THE EDUCATION OF THE FLUSHING TOILET

The community is a phenomenal resource and a great classroom. Partners must be active partners, fully involved in educating children. Don't ever ask for money from them; seek their knowledge and their support for children. One such partner was the environmental firm CH2MHill. The representative from the company was Traci (Wright) Rabindran, an African American, Harvard graduate, and engineer. Ms. Rabindran was a member of our Village Council and was eager to bring her knowledge and expertise to the children. Ms. Rabindran exemplified the ultimate partner as she first presented in the classroom and then escorted students into the community. She recalls:

I presented the wastewater treatment process to the students of MVS using a few simple household ingredients. First, I showed the students some dirty water by mixing blue food coloring and dirt in a small fish tank. This illustrated dirty influent that enters a wastewater treatment plant or, as I said to the students, "Anything that you flush down your toilet, bathtub, or sink." I placed ping-pong balls in the tank that floated to the top. This represented the scum that would sit on top of the water. Then, using an ordinary sieve from a kitchen, I removed the ping-pong balls to illustrate one of the first steps of wastewater treatment—that of removing scum from the top of a sedimentation tank.

Alum was added next, a common household ingredient used in the pickling process. The alum drew the dirt particles together and floated to the bottom. This represented bacteria that are added to dirty water sitting in a sedimentation tank in order to digest the small solids floating in the water. The bacteria sticks together and floats to the bottom of a sedimentation tank, creating sludge.

I then used a cup to remove a small sample of the dirty water. I poured the water into a funnel containing charcoal and cotton in order to filter the water. This represented the filtration process in a wastewater treatment plant. When the water passed through the homemade filter, it was no longer blue in color. Adding a small amount of household bleach to the filtered water represented the last step, chlorination. As a follow up to this demonstration, I gave the students processing sheets to review what they had learned.

The final illustration of this process was to take the students on a tour of the Jones Island Wastewater Treatment Plant, thanks to the assistance of the Milwaukee Metropolitan Sewerage District (MMSD). The experience reinforced what the students had already learned in class, and it related to their lives, since they were all residents of Milwaukee and MMSD served their area. All of the students seemed to enjoy the trip, despite the smell!

This demonstration by a professional, within the classroom, coupled with the subsequent treatment plant visit is a science lesson that students will not soon forget. This was a wonderful science classroom. Like the Energizer bunny, they kept on going and going as they went to the shores of Lake Michigan.

> *Business partners bring learning into the classroom to make it real. This is a great way to access higher-level learning from those who do it every day for a living.*

IN SEARCH OF A TEACHABLE MOMENT

Since Milwaukee is on the shore of Lake Michigan, remarkable science teacher Catherine (Hnat) Spivey took her students to the water for her project.

The students and I chose to create a Web site called "Liquid Survival," which would encompass geography, water analysis and testing, global freshwater availability, the resources from which we get freshwater, and the threats of pollution or overuse of freshwater. This was a high-level project for middle school, but the tasks were hands-on, and students were motivated by the topic.

We involved schools in the four states that surround Lake Michigan in water testing and an environmental site analysis. We all went out on the same day at the same time and performed the same tests. The data was then submitted to us from all schools to include on our Web site. The students were deeply involved in collecting samples and data and doing tests, including the dissolved oxygen tests. We even had a school in Kenya corresponding with us who wanted to do the same type of project on their lake. Students loved the project and wanted it to grow. To this day, I see former students at the mall, and they still talk about that learning experience.

Now we delve into the world of sales. We wanted to set up an African marketplace where there was high public visibility, so we called the central administration for permission to sell in front of their main office. Their response was, "If I let you do it, then everyone will want to." How wonderful! Just think of it, every day students selling items, entertaining, and celebrating learning right in front of the central administration building. Well, that administrator didn't think it was wonderful, so we moved a block away to a small park and accomplished our goal, an introduction to the world of retail sales. Art teacher Darrell Terrell tells of his efforts in the Afrocentric "Market Place":

The African purpose of a Market Day is to bring a oneness among people. That is also the purpose for our middle school students. It allows for the education of students in a holistic manner. The Market Day is a culminating activity where students demonstrate learning through a display of works and performances. The centralized theme is entrepreneurship through community, as well as social and political responsibility. Through this activity, students develop an understanding of cooperative economic systems, the importance of leadership and community service. They also develop an approach to the understanding of government. In language arts, students demonstrate reading comprehension by retelling African folklore, identifying the type of folklore and its elements, and exploring the cultural connections represented in the story. Students exhibit oral presentation skills through the use of appropriate intonation and gesture, by varying volume, and making natural eye contact. This is one of a whole range of activities where students actually open a market place, sell items, have musical performances, and practice the art of story telling. The Market Day, like our other adventures within the community, was successful and an exhilarating cultural experience.

And we continued to explore the neighborhood. When students came back from community experiences, they wrote thank-you letters. Not just because it was the right thing to do, but also because they learned from it. The letters were written correctly before they were sent out. Everyone learned how to write a proper letter, and no one complained. It just flowed as part of an overall activity.

> *The school was everywhere the children went. They learned valuable, usable information.*

EXPLORING THE UNIVERSE TO THE MOON AND BACK

When we took the classroom into the community, we asked students what experiences they wanted and where in the community they could find them. A group of students involved in an after-school club responded: horseback riding, skiing, ice skating, roller blading, hiking, rock climbing, bowling, archery, camping, flying, hang gliding, fishing, and tobogganing. They also wanted to visit various restaurants, go on a big boat in the ocean, see a whale, visit museums, fly to the moon, and live out many other wonderful dreams. It appeared we might have to expand the definition of the community a little.

Almost every student was in a formal or informal after-school group as no one had to catch the bus home. One particular group, however, consisted of the twenty-five males who needed us the most. Isn't it amazing? Some of the most difficult students were the most likely to stay around after school. The members of this group involved themselves in a range of activities, primarily focusing on preventing drug, alcohol, and tobacco abuse, with an array of community mentors lending support. The students became the planners, setting up future speakers, trips, travels, and experiences. They called their group "Dreams and Opportunities" and reverted to their list of desired experiences. A calendar was created, and the boys became involved in every aspect of the planning. As usual, parents were welcomed to all activities, and Bob's mother, Ms. Edwards, and his sister became adopted group members and participated in all activities.

With a goal of fulfilling their dreams, they met once a week after school and worked on their list and planned. They proudly designed their own T-shirts with the logo "Dream Seekers," and a cadre of adult volunteers guided them through many new experiences. Transportation became an issue as the community expanded beyond what anyone imagined. To the rescue again came our mobile partner David Crouthers. As president of D&L Bus Company, he drove often when our children were involved. Concerned for the safety of these boys after dark, David went beyond the call of duty and drove them directly to their homes, jockeying his huge coach through the narrow streets of our neighborhood. As we approached one home, the curtains parted ever so slightly. Sean thanked the driver, departed, and waved to his peers. The next day at school, Sean shared this story: "My grandmother saw the bus coming and peeked out of the window. She told the family that an important person must have been coming because there was a huge bus in front of the home. I told Grandma that I was that important person!"

Helped by a large grant and the usual group of volunteers, we boarded David's bus for the final culminating activity. We were off to see the whales. Boston, Massachusetts, was the destination, and we intended to take in every experience along the way. The bus was our classroom, and these were some of the lessons:

- Students kept a journal, completed nightly (writing).
- Students kept track of the trip on a map (reading and mapping skills).
- Students studied the states en route (social studies).
- Students learned noted historical information about Boston (social studies).
- Students estimated travel times (math).
- Students estimated the number of miles traveled (math).
- Students paid for the gas with $100 bills; they counted the change and got the receipts (math).
- Students chose places to eat based on quality and cost (decision making, math).
- Students figured out costs and paid tips (math).
- Students used the proper social skills in various places (character development).
- Students packed suitcases (spatial skills, responsibility).
- Students were responsible for their belongings (responsibility).
- Students got up on time (responsibility).

- Students packed and repacked a bus (spatial skills).
- Students got along with others for a long period of time in close quarters (character development).
- Students reported on the trip when they returned (speaking skills).
- Students wrote about the trip when they returned (writing).

Far different from memorizing irrelevant drivel and taking a multiple-choice test, these students lived their education.

We lived the dreams and what we had studied in the classroom on the bus. We visited the new Fleet Center while standing next to the old Boston Garden and ate lots of seafood at the No Name Pier. We stood in Faneuil Hall Square and talked about Thomas Jefferson, John Adams, and George Washington. We traced the route of Paul Revere and went into the Old North Church. We shared pizza and a basketball game with students at the League School of Boston and participated in a pickup game with Italian youth in Little Italy, who gifted us with a little black fish who was protected and cared for by all during the bus ride home. And yes, we did see whales. Arriving home, students were anxious to tell awaiting parents about their adventure. All were greeted with hugs by anxious parents.

They really were together in the community, and the community stretched as far as it would go. (We're still working on the moon trip.)

CHAPTER 6

Blazing the Trail

A headline in a neighborhood newspaper, the *Milwaukee Courier*, read "Precedent Setting School on Road to Success." Donna Jones authored this article about MVS and served as a substitute teacher in the school for several weeks. She saw everything there was to see. She quoted me (EL) as saying, "the initial plan will take a full three years to get everything in place, and so far, while the children are thriving, it's exhausting on teachers." The article went on to talk about the positive aspects of the school and highlighted one of our wonderful teachers, LaShawn Roscoe. Clearly, blazing the trail toward new educational frontiers is exhausting. The startup of a new school is extremely difficult when radical changes are being implemented. Especially difficult was the start-up of every year as new grade levels were added. However, I don't believe the first pioneers going to California had it too easy either; we came to know how they felt.

POWER, EGO, AND CONTROL

Clearly, we were on the road to success, but could we prevail? Essential to maintaining a new school is an agreement of support that allows it to continue over and beyond politics. Without this agreement, a school or any innovative idea is vulnerable and dependent on a particular board or superintendent. Superintendent Bob Jasna retired in 1997 and his deputy, Barbara Horton, replaced him on an interim basis for the 1997–1998 school year. A new, more conservative school board was in place, and the rhetoric of reform was slowly and surely replacing efforts at true reform. Support for our independence was dwindling and talk of a "takeover" by the high school was becoming more prevalent. The desire of self-appointed community leaders changed from keeping us out of the high school to the high school taking us over. Becoming concerned, I (EL) met with the acting superintendent, Barbara Horton. If we were going to continue with this school, the obstacles had to stop. Many issues came up in that meeting, but I left satisfied that our students had her full support.

In our third year, the 1997–1998 school year, we packed the house. We were allocated 210 students and had enrolled 237, turning down many more. With a minimal effort, we could easily have had three hundred students that year. The reputation of the school among our steadfast parents was strong, and we were growing. We had our own constructed facility within the high school, and the new high school principal was supportive. I had known Willie Jude for many years and had respect for him. When our children entered that year, he was there to welcome them. Imagine, for the first time in three years, neighborhood middle school children were welcomed to the building by the high school administrator. Not only was he a professional, he wasn't stupid. He knew those children could come to his high school in a matter of a few years. We had won over a significant number of high school staff members and outlasted a goodly number more. The high school staff was no longer a threat to us. With a supportive high school principal, we were able to access any needed facilities. The MVS staff was also growing. More educators were buying into the program. We still had some dissenters, and that was difficult every year. The teams were becoming stronger and, although it would still take a while, with support the philosophy would endure. It was then that we realized the issues were beyond the confines of the school.

Politics surrounding the high school were overwhelming and went beyond the authority of the principal. The self-appointed community leaders, along with some higher-level administrators, didn't share the professionalism of Principal Jude. Success is scary to those stuck in reverse, and saboteurs began coming out of the woodwork. New teachers, interviewed for MVS, were being sent elsewhere as a last gasp effort of the Human Resources Department to maintain its power. Money, to the tune of $42,000 left over from the MVS teacher budget, was used to fund Milwaukee Public Schools district summer school, rather than the traditional transfer to our usable budget. This was a problem with all schools, but it hit us the hardest. This was no accident, but we stayed the course. We were determined to succeed for the sake of the children, but it was getting more difficult.

> *Significant to the quest for educational reform is the fact that the keepers of the status quo become offended and retaliation occurs with a vengeance.*

PUTTING ON THE FLAK JACKET

> The trick is to get your concepts sold and implemented in the current environment and then to get the concepts installed systemwide. . . . On a more global scale, what you are trying to do needs to be put in place nationwide as an everyday way of doing business in our schools.

These words, in a letter from Guy Hoppe, personnel manager at Marquette Electronics, make clear the need for the dream of reform to spread throughout the country, if not the world. It is evident that schools around the country and beyond are struggling to serve children. It is a tall order, and we were heading in the right direction. However, with a new school board controlled by those who lacked vision, the future looked bleak. Mary Gale had seen the handwriting on the wall earlier and left. Barbara Horton was released within a few months after she started, and a new superintendent was hired, mirroring the status quo nature of the board. I (EL) was becoming "the problem" to those who would use children to further their own political agendas. The broadside attacks on me were increasing and services for our children were decreasing.

Having become part of the problem and health being an issue, I (EL) came up with a last-ditch effort to save the philosophy that was working for MVS children. In our original agreement with the school board, we were given the ability to hire our own staff, including the lead administrator. I had talked with Dr. Teretha Harper, an excellent African American principal, hoping she would be interested in the lead administrator position to keep the dream alive. She agreed.

I felt the school would be in safe hands if the school council so chose. I chose to retire from MVS at the end of the year. Even though the polling of parents indicated 100 percent wanted to remain separate from the high school, they were never really considered. When I brought this up to a high-level administrator, her response was, "What right do you have to speak for our parents"? It was clear to me that, no matter how long I stayed or whoever the high school principal was, if I were there, the failed high school would take us over. I had offended too many people by standing up for the children of our school's precious neighborhood, and the resistance toward me and the students was deeply seeded and very political.

The massive political divisions developing within the school board and promoted by self-appointed community leaders were clearly damaging to reform and children. It would be many years before we could implement the entire philosophy, and I doubted that it could be implemented at all in this large public school bureaucracy. Our only hope was that Dr. Harper, or someone of her caliber, would be able to carry on. I agreed to help, at no cost, to maintain our efforts to quash the rhetoric of reform. It was time for me to take reform to another level, a level where experiences from MVS could open the doors for other educational innovators.

It was in our original agreement, approved unanimously by the board in 1995, that new staff, including the lead administrator, would be interviewed and accepted by the school council before being hired. If we got a visionary to take the reins, the philosophy could be saved and endure until the next board or superintendent change. On May 12, 1998, Faith (Johnson) Bugg, our parent representative, and I wrote a letter to a high-ranking administrative official, with copies sent everywhere, requesting information regarding interview dates. The response was a letter telling us that they, the school district, got to choose whether the school council picked the new MVS administrator or the district did. Our sources had already told us that one of the assistant principals from the high school would be the new administrator. This would put the high school on the inside track to take over MVS, but we still held out some hope. It was late May, and we still hadn't heard anything from the district regarding administrator interviews. We were not surprised.

A grandparent visited me one day with high praise for the school and how effective we had been with her grandson. I expressed my hope that the school would remain independent of the high school in accordance with the wishes of parents and would maintain the philosophy that was becoming successful. She said she had connections with a high-ranking official and would talk to her about that thought. The next week, at the May principals' meeting, my supervisor came to me with a message from the previously mentioned official. "You will cease and desist talking to parents about . . . [that school]." Unbelievable! Principal Ken Holt was sitting nearby, and we looked at each other in total disbelief. I had been ordered by a high-ranking Milwaukee public school official to stop talking to our parents about the future of the school! Of course, I didn't cease and desist anything. Rather than choose someone who was in tune with our philosophy, an individual was selected whose allegiance was with the high school. It was clear that the high school assistant principal was my replacement.

> *Reform was systematically and intentionally halted. The high school assistant principal, used as the pawn, replaced me at MVS. The Milwaukee system simply didn't care about MVS parents.*

MOVING ON

It was time to implement as much of the original philosophy as we could before I (EL) left. We designed a plan that allowed movement through the school system. An eleven-year-old through completion design appeared to be the easiest way to accomplish this goal; however, reality dictated differently. Our third year was at hand, and we hadn't been given approval to start our fourth level as per our proposal, so we began to prepare students for the transition to a traditional high school. With Mr. Jude as principal at North Division High School, we encouraged our students to attend there so they could remain in the familiar building. That was one of the promises we had made to the neighborhood parents. Many students chose a different school, as they clearly remembered their poor treatment by some high school staff members. For those who were interested in staying, Mr. Jude and I developed a creative plan. North Division High School's curriculum was divided into trimesters, starting in September, late November, and March. We reached an agreement that when our students were ready, they could move up to the high school at any of those three times. If students were not ready in June, they had the option of reaching it in November or March. At least students would not fail and go back to repeat the entire year.

The first pioneers tested the waters when they moved to North Division High School in late March. Two of those five MVS students made the honor roll immediately, and a new era had begun. Willie Monroe was among the five who became high school students early, and he was excited. He wanted to be the first of the MVS students to graduate from North Division High School. This would give him the distinction of being the first student to complete both middle and high school in the same building.

TAKING PRIDE

The first pioneers blazed the trails, but not everyone made it to California. They did, however, clear the way for others who would have never made it otherwise. We took pride, first and foremost, in the children we had influenced. So many had developed the joy of learning. We also took pride in our accomplishments and the opportunities we had afforded others. We celebrate those ideas that ended up as change on a more systemic scale. Reform comes slowly in a large urban school system, and as a catalyst for change, we opened the door for others. Here are some of the changes consistent with our philosophy:

• *The proficiency concept*: This concept, adopted by Milwaukee Public Schools in 1997 and implemented in 2000, was supported when superintendent Dr. Spence Korte announced that students would no longer be promoted to high school based on letter grades. Dr. Cynthia Ellwood helped MVS in the development of this process and then was instrumental in expanding the concept to all middle schools. Warnings to us by author Jonathon Kozol that these proficiencies would soon turn into rigid standards came true. In time, we can only hope that proficiencies will redevelop into the classroom-based guidelines and individual demonstrations of learning they were intended to be.

- *Accessing the community*: This was made easier systemwide, as schools become able to extend their classrooms into the community with one parent signature on an emergency contact card at the beginning of the year.
- *Site-based staff interviews*: Following the lead of Hi Mount School principal Dr. Spence Korte and MVS, all schools in the Milwaukee system are now able to interview and hire their own staff. The stranglehold of the once powerful Human Resources Department has been broken.
- *Staff racial-balance requirements*: This requirement for all schools was lifted. It is a difficult concept because there still needs to be a racial balance of staff in schools, but schools with a strong minority population are now able to hire teachers who can best relate to the students and the neighborhood.
- *Year-round schools*: Through the hard work and support of then deputy superintendent Tom McGinnity, the willing staff at the payroll department facilitated a new computer program. The Payroll Department can now handle year-round school programming and pay teachers appropriately. Started by Congress Street School and attempted by MVS, this ability is now firmly in place. Our good friend, principal Martha Wheeler-Fair, was the first to take her elementary school in that direction. A middle school, Milwaukee Education Center, followed suit, and there are more to come.
- *The Milwaukee Board of School Directors Innovative Schools Committee*: This committee, developed in 1995 as a vehicle for new ideas, led to the acceptance of charter schools inside the Milwaukee system. In addition, school educators now have a vehicle to get their innovative ideas heard. This committee is still in place today.
- *Charter schools within the Milwaukee public schools*: The five initial innovative schools led the way to the acceptance of charter schools within the public system. Although many have been diminished to simply a different form of site-based management, they are poised to jump into action and develop innovative philosophies at any time.

- *Community learning centers (CLCs)*: These CLCs sprouted up everywhere with the aid of a federal grant and a major federal initiative. Their design was just as we had hoped. The National Community Education Association was the driving force behind these centers, and Milwaukee is in the lead. This concept, shared by the original philosophy of the Milwaukee Village School and Community Center, led to extended learning within schools.
- *Federal Title 1 money availability for year one*: As a new school, MVS was denied per-child Title 1 money during our first year due to the rules of implementation. Adjustments have been made to overcome this and allow new schools similar funding the first year.
- *School within a school*: Several "school within a school" designs have been implemented since our attempt in 1995. Administrators have learned from our efforts. This is significant because a dramatic increase in the implementation of this concept appears to be in the near future across the nation.
- *Neighborhood Schools Initiative*: In 1995, MVS was the only neighborhood middle school in the Milwaukee system. Since that time, the Milwaukee School Board has adopted a Neighborhood Schools Initiative with the intent of dramatically increasing the number of neighborhood schools. This process is moving forward, but has a long way to go.
- *Assessment process*: An assessment process that holds schools accountable for the students they have was adapted by the charter school assessment committee to assess Milwaukee-area charter schools. This concept was everyday business at MVS. In addition to systemic change within the school system, some major developments have occurred, supported by involvement with our business partners:
- *MATA Media Communications*: Director Vel Wiley, speaking to MVS students April and Chante, said, "It was . . . the success of you ladies . . . that really led to our ability to get a grant and create a formal education access department that works solely with youth. Because you demonstrated the importance and value that comes out of it."
- *The Farm City Link project*: Will Allen, speaking to MVS student Willie Monroe, said:

The initial work with you guys gave me a lot of . . . inspiration because of what I saw, what you guys got out of it. This has become . . . a meaningful part of my life. Our program is now multigenerational working with young people, adults, and elders, passing on information to the whole community. It's something that has become an inspirational part of my life, it's what I do.

- *Readers Choice Bookstore*: Carla Allison, speaking to MVS students April and Chante, said, "I have had several schools come in and ask about a book club, and your school is always the model I use. It's a model I recommend because it works so smoothly. It was a delightful experience and is something I continue to share with other schools."

AULD LANG SYNE

The year ended well. The last of the yearly camping trips was wonderful. This, the third one for the graduates, had them bonding amazingly well. The traditional snipe hunt was completed, and although they may have sensed fraud, they never let on. We stopped in a clearing and again talked about the North Star and followed the drinking gourd back to the cottages. When we were done, I (EL) pulled out my guitar and everyone sang "This Little Light of Mine." I mean literally *everyone* sang. Usually, there will be a couple on the side talking and a few more walking around. Not with this group; they all sang as one. It was wonderful.

Our time was ending, and the promotion ceremony was the final salute to this wonderful group of children, most of whom had been with us the entire three years. We didn't even try to get a guest speaker, because this was my time to tell them once more, "Never forget how wonderful you are." The place was packed with every parent we had ever met, and they responded when I asked how many had been with us for the entire three years. Most of them had. We reminisced about meeting them in their living rooms when we were going door-to-door recruiting students. Afterward, children told stories about trips and exhibitions and camping and on and on. When the day was over, the year was over, and I quietly slipped into retirement. I felt happy for the children we had influenced, but beaten for not being able to finish what we had started, for not being able to inspire another group of wonderful children.

Everyone was tired from the unbelievably long year. I wondered why so many people didn't want our children and our program to succeed. Very few knew what had really transpired at the Milwaukee Village School and Community Center. So many only wanted to see failure, and they looked for and found their own favorite answer. They weren't looking when Sunny learned to read, or when Germaine saw the whales, or when April wrote a poem, or when Prince presented to college students or when . . .

Education is not about standardized tests. It is about inspiring children to achieve the joy of learning. Once they get the joy of learning, nothing can stop them from succeeding. As they walked across the stage, they handed us their completed portfolios, showing that they had learned. We, in turn, handed them a certificate of promotion, acknowledging this.

THE TIMES THEY ARE A-CHANGIN'

The following years led to many changes in MVS. Our philosophy was replaced by that of the failed high school. The official proclamation that the two schools were combining would come soon. On my last day, the new administrator told me, as a high school staff member carried away our computer server, "we are one school with the high school now." The class design was changed; no longer were there four teachers for two classes. One team was set up with four classes, all in separate subject areas, and students moved from class to class, just like high school. They followed the textbook and received letter grades: As and Bs for students in English, even those who were reading on the second- and third-grade level. The school wasn't a neighborhood school anymore. Disciplinary problems, being referred from other schools, came to MVS, regardless of where they lived in the city. Soon, they became the dominant population. There were no exhibitions or demonstrations of learning and only an occasional community experience.

Art specialty was dropped due to low enrollment, and, according to a teacher, the reading assessment indicated that less than 15 percent of all students improved their reading in the 1999–2000 school year. This figure was well below the 75 percent of our children who had improved their reading in the 1997–1998 school year. That included all students, even those with special education needs. The average 85 percent attendance throughout the first three years turned into a record-setting 88.9 percent truancy in 2002, according to an article in the *Milwaukee Journal-Sentinel*, the worst in the city among middle schools. Boys were separated from girls in all classes for supposed better behavior, while the Village Square became a detention area for disruptive children. The breakout rooms, which once housed students in small groups in the square, now housed offices, one adult per room, and students with special education needs had their status branded on their foreheads again and were separated from the other students. Decisions were once more made without surveying the parents. While visiting there one day, I was told by a staff member that they had to hurry and call a parent meeting to approve the union of the high school and middle school. It appeared the decision was already made. This is how schools "end-run" parents. According to a staff member, the hurry-up meeting was held with a small number of MVS parents, but dominated by the high school parents, and the coup was complete.

It took four years to plan and break through barriers and three years to implement the program, but only fifteen minutes to break it down.

In April 1999, our first year away from the school, an election was held, and there was a massive changing of the guard on the school board. We weren't sure whether this new board would be better in the long run, but they took swift action. Within months, the superintendent and his team were dismissed, and the new administration was in place. This administration was more favorable to efforts like ours, but its hands appeared to be tied. It did take a few more steps toward reform. Three years later, in August of 2002, there was yet another administrative change, with new superintendent Bill Andrekoupolis taking charge. There is no telling when he will be replaced and if his efforts will be erased. More and more educators, however, are looking at real reform and are beginning to embrace it, one small step at a time. It is a slow, cumbersome process, and MVS was at the cutting edge.

THE NEW PIONEERS

Hope still exists, and a group of new pioneers is making its mark on history. A grassroots organization from around the country called ACT NOW 2003, under the leadership of author Susan Ohanian, is exposing the fallacy of one singular standardized test determining the success or failure of students. A founding member, Dr. Bill Cala, the superintendent from Fairport, New York, is doing his part. He presented three courageous resolutions that his school board passed. The resolutions called on the state to rescind all unfunded mandates passed since 1995, to rescind all commissioner's regulations since 1995, and to require the superintendent to return the state's high-stakes tests to the commissioner ungraded. The Fairport School Board passed these resolutions unanimously, and on March 19, 2003, the concerns went to the state, and Bill still has his job.

Two Texas bills presented by state representative Dora Olivo are introducing legislation that allow for multiple measures in assessing Texas students. House Bill (HB) 336 calls for TAKS (the Texas State standardized test) exit tests to be used as one of several multiple compensatory criteria and HB337 calls for multiple compensator criteria in the making of promotion and retention decisions in the third grade. Carol Holst is promoting sound education as an ACT NOW 2003 member in Texas. This is just a beginning as the dominoes begin to fall, leading to the ultimate goal of teaching the whole child, one step at a time. Gloria Pipkin is leading the charge in Florida as president of the Florida Coalition for Assessment Reform. This grassroots not-for-profit organization provides resources and assistance to parents, teachers, students, and other citizens who support constructive assessment. With ReLeah Lent, Pipkin coauthored *At the Schoolhouse Gate: Lessons in Intellectual Freedom.* In the state of Washington, a parent, Juanita Doyan, is running for state superintendent when she is not making buttons for ACT NOW. She authored the book *Not with Our Kids You Don't.* Judi Hirsch in California, Sue Allison in Maryland, Dave Stratman in Massachusetts, and people all over the country are working for the common goal of quashing the rhetoric of reform, while moving forward with real reform.

When attention is given to the new pioneers, they are seen sprouting up everywhere. Steve Orel in Birmingham, Alabama, is working hard, teaming with the older students who need us the most. The school is called the World of Opportunity (WOO) and is located in a one-floor cinder block structure with an attached trailer, across the road from a large public-housing project with a primarily African American population on the outskirts of Birmingham. The students range in age and include sixteen-year-olds and senior citizens; many live within walking distance of the school. As soon as you walk into the WOO, you are struck by the warm glow of humanity that comes from every inch of wall space being covered with pictures of WOO students and messages celebrating their many accomplishments.

This innovative school is intergenerational; young and old students interact with each other and the roles they play in making WOO work. For example, Lucille is a student at WOO and is sharpening her reading skills in preparation for the GED exam. She is also a mentor to the younger students and is a member of the WOO Advisory Board. Although the ultimate goal is passing the GED, education at this school goes well beyond preparing for that test. Teaching the whole student at the WOO puts a strong reality focus on the needs of the students and provides a true investment in their future.

An example of integrating the arts with education is seen at Stanton Elementary School in the Kentucky mountains, according to Robert Cornet of Georgetown, Kentucky. Robert has been a small businessman, a state budget director, an author, and organizer of a bluegrass festival he calls a Celebration of Music and Learning. Stanton School provides the teaching of bluegrass music after school, using adult volunteers and student graduates of the program to help kids learn through music. The only thing left to do is to make this part of the daily school program, instead of an after-school adventure in learning.

David Powell at Milwaukee's Vincent High School also has a school/after-school program that would make a wonderful public school/charter school. David uses theater arts, forensics, and community experiences to educate over one hundred African American students. All students, even those with special education needs, are fully involved in this real learning process. In addition, the students go to other schools to teach forensics. Language and reading skills have skyrocketed for these youth beyond those in the rest of the school. Students with special education needs are included in the program and all testing.

Meanwhile, Theresa Erbe from Fritsche Middle School in Milwaukee is working to open a small Milwaukee public high school called the Professional Learning Institute. She already has her students landscaping the court area of the school, learning leadership skills, while bonding with each other before her school opens. Another courageous teacher, Valerie Benton-Davis, has the energy to start a new school designed to serve students who need us the most, pregnant teenage girls. I (EL) especially commend her for knocking on doors to find students and respecting the skills and abilities of all. Every student has a flame to nurture, and Northern Star School, Milwaukee Public Schools, appears to be on the way to fueling that flame. New Milwaukee superintendent Bill Andrekoupolis is working hard to bring the spirit of innovation to this public school system not only by making high schools smaller, but also by making them different, designed to meet students' needs. With the support of another pioneer, Wisconsin state superintendent Dr. Elizabeth Burmaster, hope remains strong. It's a difficult task, but the hope is held by new pioneers all over the country. The way was paved in Milwaukee when one superintendent responded to one letter back in 1991. The way is now being paved everywhere.

> *Yes, not all pioneers made it to California. Some just blazed the trail for others. It is the duty of the new pioneers to carry on and make the dream real, for the sake of the children.*

Keep reminding others and have them keep reminding you about who matters. We always tried to keep our focus on the students, and when we slipped, there was someone there to remind us. Not everyone will be supportive. Some will attack you with every fiber of their being. Just remember who matters, and you will prevail if your hearts are for the children. When you ask people about MVS, you will hear, "Great things happened there," or you will hear, "Wow, that was a bad school." Rarely will you hear anything in between. It all depends on the agenda of the person you are talking to, whether they believe in real reform for children or they are simply talking the rhetoric of reform. Just remember who matters: those who talk rhetoric or the children?

You have just read the rough-and-tumble story of how we started MVS. The obstacles will continue to be extreme, but if enough of us take the challenge, the winds of change will blow dramatically across the country. Teachers will begin to teach to the children again, and children will progress at their best rates in their desired directions. Under the watchful eye of educators and parents, children will not be left behind, forgotten in a crowd. Their progress will be monitored, and their hopes and dreams kept alive.

Now it's your time to take action. In the words of activist Bobby Seals, "If not now, when?" It's your time to quash the rhetoric of reform. Our focus is urban, but the ideas can be replicated in any part of this country, be it urban, rural, or suburban. They can also be replicated anywhere in the world and beyond.

To do this we must build small schools or change existing ones throughout the world. Now it's your turn to go to the moon.

NEW TOMORROWS
Is your son or your daughter a part of a village?
Surrounded by people who care.
Encouraged to look far beyond the horizon,
Protected from cynical snare
Tomorrow won't grow from this standardized testing
Anymore than the tide rules the sea
It comes when you nurture the flame in each child,
Tests don't show what tomorrow can be.
Shatter the locks that prevent bright tomorrows.
Tear down those walls make them free!
When the parent, the village and teacher unite,
It's the child that achieves victory!

Words, music by George Swanson
Inspired by the Milwaukee Village School and Community Center © 2003

Bibliography

Anderson, James. *School, the Story of American Public Education*. Princeton, N.J.: Films for the Humanities and Sciences, 2001. Videocassette.

Armstrong, Thomas. *Multiple Intelligences in the Classroom*. Alexandria, Va.: Association for Supervision and Curriculum Development, 1994.

Bledsoe, Lucy Jane. *Caught Reading*. Paramus, N.J.: Globe Feron Educational, 1995.

Brigance, Albert H. *Comprehensive Inventory of Basic Skills*. North Billerica, Mass.: Curriculum Associates, 1983.

Chandler, Merrill, et al. *Milwaukee Innovative Schools, Case Descriptions*. Oakbrook, Ill.: North Central Regional Educational Laboratory, United States Department of Education, 1996.

Cornett, Robert M. *Is It Time for a Grandparents Manifesto?* Georgetown, Ky.: SixSons Press, 2002.

Doyan, Juanita. *Not with Our Kids You Don't*. Portsmouth, N.H.: Heinemann, 2003.

Evans, Joyce. "Young Poet Is on the Ball, in Life and Sports." *Milwaukee Journal-Sentinel*, 14 April 1997, 1B.

Gardner, Howard. *Frames of Mind*. New York: Basic Books, 1983.

Goldman, Gary, and Jay Newman. *Empowering Students to Transform Schools*. Thousand Oaks, Calif.: Corwin Press, 1998.

Goldstein, Arnold P., et al. *Skillstreaming the Adolescent*. Champaign, Ill.: Research Press, 1980.

Grove, Vicki, *The Crystal Gardens*. New York: Putnam, 1995.

Herndon, James. *The Way It Spozed to Be*. Portsmouth, N.H.: Heinemann, 1999.

Hockett, Lorna. "Who's in the Bag?" in *Teacher Talk*. vol. 3. Bloomington, Ind.: Indiana University, 1995.

Jones, Donna. "Precedent Setting School on Road to Success." *Milwaukee Courier*, 23 November 1996, 5.

Junior Great Books. Chicago: Great Books Foundation, 1984.

Kipling, Rudyard. "Letting in the Jungle," *Junior Great Books*. Chicago: Great Books Foundation, 1992.

Macaulay, David. *Motel of the Mysteries*. Boston: Houghton Mifflin, 1979.

Mead, Margaret. *Growing Up in New Guinea*. New York: William & Morrow, 1953.

Merrow, John. *Choosing Excellence: "Good Enough" Schools Are Not Good Enough*. Lanham, Md.: Scarecrow Press, 2001.

Ohanian, Susan. *Is That Penguin Stuffed or Real?* Bloomington, Ind.: *Phi Delta Kappan*, 1996.

Pipkin, Gloria, and ReLeah Lent. *At the Schoolhouse Gate: Lessons in Intellectual Freedom*. Portsmouth, N.H.: Heinemann, 2002.

Pino, Ed., *Remaking Our Schools*. Menomonie, Wis.: IGS, 1993.

Schulhofer-Whol, Sam. "MPS Truancy Hits 40%." *Milwaukee Journal-Sentinel*, 5 February 2002, 1A, 12A.

Smith, Nila Banton. *Be a Better Reader*. Upper Saddle River, N.J.: Globe Feron Educational Publishers, 1997.

Tuckman, B. W. "Developmental Sequence in Small Groups." *Psychological Bulletin* 63 (1965): 384–399.

About the Authors

Eldon Lee has spent thirty years teaching regular and special education students. He graduated from Eastern Michigan University in Ypsilanti, Michigan, with a BS in health, physical education, and recreation. After working in a residential treatment center near Detroit, he moved to Milwaukee, Wisconsin, to become a physical education teacher at Pleasant View School in the Milwaukee public school system. His interest in all children led him to get his MA in special education at Cardinal Stritch College and teach in that field. In addition to teaching, he coached boys' high school baseball and girls' basketball, as well as running a variety of recreation programs. He has been continually involved in professional organizations, presiding over several.

After fifteen years of teaching, Eldon got his administrative certification from the University of Wisconsin, Milwaukee, and went on to be an administrator at the high school and middle school levels, as well as lead administrator at an alternative school and, of course, starting the new innovative Milwaukee Village School with Mary Gale Budzisz. He attributes his creativity to connecting with teachers who have a strong focus on children and aren't afraid to hang onto every child until he or she learns. Although Eldon claims to be retired, he continues to advocate for children. He strongly supports those interested in real reform and is willing to help any school that truly wants to change the way we think about how we educate children.

Mary Gale Budzisz is an internationally known educator who has spent thirty-one years teaching regular and special education students.

She graduated from Mankato State Teachers College in Mankato, Minnesota, with a BS in physical education and health education. She then moved to Milwaukee, Wisconsin, to become a physical education teacher at Solomon Juneau High School in the Milwaukee public school system. In addition, she became the first woman coach in the Milwaukee school system, where she coached boys' tennis. Mary Gale developed an interest in special education early in her career and got her MS in that area from the University of Wisconsin, Milwaukee. She has gone on to become a widely acclaimed teacher, having received both local and national awards for her efforts, as well as presiding over eleven professional organizations from the local to the international level.

Mary Gale says much of her success is due to the fact that she has worked with intelligent principals who gave her the latitude to be a creative, innovative practitioner. This freedom allowed her to adapt materials, methods, and techniques to promote success for each student. She has never wanted to do anything other than teach, as she is adamant about the success of her students. Although Mary Gale claims to be retired, she's constantly on the move, kayaking near her home in South Carolina or running an international conference in Australia. Her sincere support of children, as well as her dynamic speaking ability, has made her a highly sought-after retiree.